In memory of
VEN. DR. K SRI DHAMMANANDA

You & Your PROBLEMS

VEN. DR. K SRI DHAMMANANDA

Published by

BUDDHIST MISSIONARY SOCIETY MALAYSIA
123, Jalan Berhala,
50470 Kuala Lumpur,
Malaysia
Tel: (603) 22741889/1886
Fax: (603) 22733835
Email: bmsm@po.jaring.my

1st Edition 31 Jan 2004 - 10,000 copies
ISBN 983-40071-2-4
©*2004 K Sri Dhammananda*

Reprinted and Donated for free distribution by
The Corporate Body of the Buddha Educational Foundation
11F., 55 Hang Chow South Road Sec 1, Taipei, Taiwan, R.O.C.
Tel: 886-2-23951198 , Fax: 886-2-23913415
Email: overseas@budaedu.org
Website: http: //www.budaedu.org
This book is strictly for free distribution, it is not for sale.

CONTENTS

THE ROLE OF RELIGION

THE SELF AND FAMILY

MAN AND SOCIETY

THE CORRECT ATTITUDE

FOREWORD

In more than half a century of Buddhist educational activities in Malaysia and Singapore Venerable Dr. K. Sri Dhammananda has shared his wider knowledge of the Teachings of the Buddha with countless thousands of people all over the world through his sermons as well as his numerous publications. The appeal of his style of preaching lies in the fact that he has consistently made the ancient Teachings delivered in India 25 centuries ago directly relevant to people in the present day world. No one can deny that while the Teachings are timeless, they nevertheless have to be re-interpreted to suit the vastly different mentalities of the people of the world today. While the human condition remains unchanged, the people of today live under circumstances which are so different that they need the assistance of capable monks like Venerable Dhammananda to help them cope with present day problems in keeping with the Buddha's advice.

Besides being a Dharma teacher, Venerable Dhammananda has also given invaluable service as a counsellor of one who applies his vast knowledge to help people come to terms with suffering and to understand the problems of daily living. This present book is yet another effort by the Venerable to record in writing these valuable words of wisdom so that they can reach a larger section of humanity the world over. The Venerable has included some of the materials which he used in previous publications but it also includes a great deal of new material to address problems which surfaced in recent years.

The Venerable's books are being read world wide because they are written in simple language and are directly focused on the challenges presented by modern civilization. He avoids clumsy quotations in Pali and he does not distract the reader with lengthy quotations from little known texts. Having been closely associated with people from all walks of life and with different religions persuasions, he is amply qualified to answer their questions and remove their doubts.

In this book the author uses the word 'man' referring to human beings regardless of gender. Also, the book has been organized under a variety of subheadings to cover a wide range of subjects. They have been loosely assembled together into five separate sections, although they are not mutually exclusive. This is because the author hopes the book will be used as a constant reference to which the reader will return very often. Ideally the book should be read a little at a time with plenty of room to ponder over each item and to consider the problem of human existence.

Vijaya Samarawickrama

Acknowledgement

We wish to express our sincere thanks and appreciation to Mr. Vijaya Samarawickrama, Prof. Lily de Silva, Ms. Sumana Sin and Sukhi Hotu for their assistance in one way or other without which the book would not have been possible.

Publishers

1

PROBLEMS – THEIR NATURE AND CAUSE

What is the cause of our problems?

It is impossible for any human being to exist without facing problems in this world. It is due to our ignorance of the cause of our problems that we are entangled in various disturbances from birth up to the last breath. The Buddha advised us that if we want to overcome problems we must understand their nature and origin.

He also advised us to ponder on the purpose of our existence and try to find out why we have to face so many problems. In reality there are no problems in this world but by mistaking 'the unreal for the real' or taking natural occurrences seriously into the mind we create enormous problems for everybody and for ourselves because we never think that it is natural for many of those natural occurrences to be not in our favour.

If we can understand the cause of our problems then there can be no reason for us to suffer from undue fear, worries and insecurity. Everybody likes to live a very happy and peaceful life but how many of us can really say that we experience peace in our life? We are willing to do anything in every possible way to gain a few moments of happiness, but somehow whatever happiness we gain is fleeting, never lasting for any appreciable length of time.

But lasting happiness is possible even in this lifetime if we can understand the secret of how to attain it. Because we do not understand the nature and cause of our suffering, we usually create new problems while trying to solve the existing ones, just like a lion which gets more entangled in a net when it struggles harder to escape.

If the new problem is a minor one, we tolerate it to the best of our ability and do what we can to alleviate the suffering. For example, when we have gastric ulcers and suffer severe pain, we consult a doctor. If the doctor says we have to undergo an operation, we will accept the fact that we will have to suffer more pain if we have to do it. Since we know there is no other solution, we decide to face the new problem of the operation to get rid of the existing problem.

Then we make up our mind to bear the pain and uneasiness during the operation by thinking that we can finally get rid of the pain. In the same manner we are willing to tolerate certain problems or pain to overcome the existing big problems. That is why we sometimes face the pain with a smiling face.

We cannot overcome an existing problem without facing another problem or without sacrificing something physically or mentally. It is impossible to settle our problems by being stubborn, that is why we seek a compromise and adopt a give and take policy to settle many of our problems. Patience and tolerance can help us to avoid so many problems. If we reduce our selfish ego we get the chance to avoid conflicts, clashes, enmity and violence.

The Buddha has introduced a very meaningful and practical method to settle our problems. He did not recommend a method just to patch up a problem here and there, simply to make us happy for the time being. Rather he taught us the way to penetrate to the root of the problem and to find out the main cause of it.

His method was not even to reduce the symptom of the problem like some doctors do when they cure only the symptom of our sickness but not the sickness itself. When we have a serious headache, we take some pain killer tablets and after that we feel better for a short period but it is not the complete cure because the pain can come back again. Such medicines give us temporary relief from the pain, but do not eradicate the cause of the pain itself.

Assume that we have a very painful wound in our body. After taking many kinds of medicines we may manage to cure it, and when somebody asks us how we feel, we say we are very much better. But 'better' is a relative term. Here it means that there is no more pain for the time being. For anything in this world we say we feel good or nice only to tell others there is no problem for the moment. That is why when someone asks, 'How are you?' we say 'Oh, I am fine'. But we all know that we do not speak in an absolute sense. We know very well that at any time we can be afflicted by similar or totally new kinds of pain. The physical body itself creates enormous problems. Throughout our lifetime we try to attend to them by neglecting our important duties. But the more we attend to them, the more new problems disturb us. Therefore it is an endless battle.

The Buddha's method is not to apply soothing balms to effect temporary cures, but to uproot the main cause of our problems. That is why some people say it is difficult to practice the Buddha's teaching.

On one occasion the Buddha declared that all our sufferings are caused by our getting entangled in a tangle of worldly problems. By realizing the real nature of life a person develops *sila*, which is moral behaviour or self-discipline. *Sila* means discipline of the senses, according to a moral form. A diligent and wise person knows how to trace the root of problems and overcome at least some of them.

Here the Buddha's advice for us is to be good, diligent and act wisely if we want to solve our problems. There is no other method to practice to gain a final solution to our problems. Usually whenever we have problems we approach others and seek their advice. They may ask us to go and pray to certain gods in a temple or some other places of worship. However this is not the Buddha's way. He advised us to approach the problems directly by analyzing them and finding out where they originated. We usually tend to quickly put the blame on others. If we are honest with ourselves we can trace the source of problems by ourselves. Remember the saying that when we point one finger at others, three fingers are pointing back at us. In every good action there is bad effect also. At the same time in every bad action there is some good too. *'There can be no rainbow without a cloud and a storm.'*

The trouble with us is that whenever we face any problem, we suffer even more by creating imaginary enemies and suspicion. We even seek some advise from others in order to get rid of the problems. But we do not consider that the advice that we get from others can also be based on their superstitious beliefs or imagination or wrong understanding of the problem. This is particularly true when we consider how people run to fortune-tellers and clairvoyants to solve their problems.

For example when people complain about failure in their business and bad luck, they try to use magic power to have good luck and success. The Buddha advised us to overcome problems in reasonable ways and to develop our understanding without depending on superstitious belief and to use full effort and knowledge without wasting time and money on meaningless practices.

There are people who seem to be very willing to follow those who claim that they have magical powers, supernatural powers and healing powers and they pay big sums of money to these people to bring them good luck and success. Of course, eventually, they find that they have been cheated as it is not that easy to get good fortune. And because they do not get what they want, they bring more problems to themselves. We cannot understand the cause of many of our problems because our way of thinking is generally based on ignorance which is the cause of imagination or illusion.

We do not allow ourselves to develop our way of life through proper understanding. In many ways religion can help us to develop that understanding because religion explains human nature and how to deal with problems. However many people think that religion is only for us to pray or to perform certain rituals. When we maintain such a naive attitude, how can we enrich our knowledge to understand things in their proper prospective? We do not recognize the value of religion to help us to gain happiness. Today we have organised our worldly life in such a way that we have no time to devote for mental training for peace.

The result is that although we may have more than enough to satisfy our material needs we are never satisfied and all the while we go on thinking how to make more money, how to have more sensual pleasure even at the cost of others' lives. Such pleasures are short-lived. We lose interest as soon as we have gained something we have craved for. The result is that we are constantly yearning for more of the same thing and constantly remaining unsatisfied. When we experience certain problems we start to grumble, show our temper and create more disturbances and blame others for our problems.

Today we think that people in developed countries are happy because they have so many material comforts, but the fact is that in many ways they are unhappier than people in undeveloped countries and are especially victims of mental problems. This is because they have become slaves to their sensual pleasure and crave for worldly enjoyment without proper moral development. Tension, fear, anxiety and insecurity disturb their minds. This kind of mental disturbance disturbs the human way of life.

This state of affairs has become the biggest problem in many industrialized countries because they have not learned to maintain contentment. Many people suffer from loss of confidence and face difficulties in deciding what to do with their lives. The main cause of this mental attitude is ambition and anxiety, created by competition, jealousy and fear. But these people are not only a nuisance to themselves but to those around them as well. Such problems naturally create a very bad atmosphere for others who want to lead a peaceful life. There is no short cut for us to get rid of our problems.

We must try to understand and to find out the cause of the problems that we are facing. But let us not be misled into thinking that happiness is easy to achieve because it is true that there is no life without problems. Whether we make ourselves more miserable or not depends on how much we allow our minds to affect us. As soon as some problems arise some people immediately suspect that others might have done some charms or black magic to disturb their family. But they are not ready to admit their own weaknesses to think that they themselves have contributed something to become the cause of the problems.

People live in the darkness of ignorance by not knowing what is right and what is wrong. They are struggling in the mire of worldly evils. They think that the few fleeting moments of pleasure that they may enjoy in this world are permanent; though in reality, they are impermanent.

By not understanding this glaring fact people become engrossed in pleasures of short duration and get themselves entangled in them more and more, becoming enslaved to them and thereby become totally blind to reality. To be wise among the ignorant, to be strong of heart among the weak-hearted, to be patient among the impatient, to be sober among the passion-intoxicated, to be kind among the haters, are some of the difficult achievements in our lives.

People have never experienced such phenomenal material progress as they are enjoying in this age. However, despite this wonderful progress, it is most unfortunate that mankind tends to neglect its spiritual well-being. Mankind appears to have been blinded by material achievements thinking that materialism is the end of all things.

They have forgotten that materialism alone does not provide the true happiness. They must seek true happiness and spiritual well-being through their respective religions to complement their search for happiness through materialism. Spiritual solace and materialism go hand in hand to provide true happiness for all.

Moral degradation exists everywhere. With increased efficiency of modern mass communications, we have become much more aware of man's inhumanity to man on a scale unheard of hitherto. Individuals tend to forget or completely ignore their obligations and duties to the society in which they live. Business organisations, in their ruthless scramble for profits and material gain, are pursuing their efforts without any sense of decency. They have forgotten that there is such a thing as human dignity. In the light of such a catastrophic situation, many people concerned with the upholding of human dignity and ethical practices, are tempted to throw up their hands in sheer despair of ever finding a solution to curb inordinate human greed and to steer them along the path of human decency coupled with spiritual solace.

Human beings have conquered space; they are even trying to elevate themselves to the level of super beings, but they have not been capable of conducting themselves as decent human beings with spiritual love and compassion for others. This sad state of affairs prevails today because people have chosen to take the wrong path in developing modern civilization. They have taken materialism in the mistaken belief that materialism alone can bring happiness. This is a fallacy. They have gone wrong because they have willfully chosen to ignore the invaluable advice given by our spiritual leaders over the centuries.

Whilst it is admitted that science can produce quick results and a measure of material gain, the resultant benefits from such material gain are illusory and short-lived. As against such illusory and short-lived gains, the benefits that we derive by following the noble teachings of our religious leaders are those of real lasting happiness and not illusory. Material gain without spiritual solace does not provide true and lasting happiness.

Spiritual backing is absolutely necessary for man's spiritual upliftment, leading to tranquility of mind and everlasting happiness. If we study world history concerning human behaviour in the past, we will readily agree that modern human moral conduct is not better than that of our ancestors although we pretend to glorify our civilization.

Another important aspect of Buddhism is the explanation of the main cause of human problems and sufferings. According to the Buddha, we face the problems of this mundane world due to the strong selfish craving which exists in our minds. He has revealed that there are three kinds of craving forces in our minds. These are:- craving for existence, craving for worldly or sensual indulgence, and craving for non-existence. These three cravings are responsible for our existence, our rebirth, and all the thousands of other problems and mental disturbances.

To understand the profound meaning of Buddha's interpretation, it has to be considered very wisely. Only then can realization come. World famous philosophers and psychologists have also explained these three forces, but they used different terms. The German writer Arthur Schopenhauer explained these three forces as sexuality, self-preservation and suicide.

The Austrian psychologist Sigmund Freud explained these same things as libido, ego instinct and death instinct. It was Freud's famed student Carl Jung who said, 'From the sources of instinct spring forth everything creative.'

This is the way great intellectuals are prepared to support the truth revealed by the Buddha twenty-five centuries ago. But when we study the explanations of these modern thinkers we can see that the Buddha went far beyond their understanding capacity.

Some of our problems are natural

It is true that we have to face problems throughout our lives and there is no way to avoid them. We cannot avoid disease, old age and death, for example. However, some problems are man-made, created by people according to their worldly understanding of life. Some problems are mind-made resulting from delusion, ignorance, suspicions and fear.

Mental imbalances, which we regard as madness, is another big problem. By violating an ethical way of life man disturbs his own peace and happiness and that of others. Then by allowing internal and external stimuli to affect the mind, more unsatisfactoriness, misery, excitement, fear and insecurity are created.

The world is full of disappointment. Things do not happen as we wish them to. This being so we must train ourselves to face any situation with fortitude. We may not be able to change them but certainly we can change ourselves. If a thing is unalterable then there is no alternative but to submit to it or maintain a happy sense of resignation at the inevitable. But this is not fatalistic. We accept unsatisfactory experiences because we understand the nature of life, that things cannot always work in our favour. This creates serenity in our minds.

This does not mean that we should simply bow to all the adversities that come our way. As long as there is a chance that we can change a situation in our favour let us try; but when common sense tells us that we are up against something that is the way it is, and cannot be otherwise, then let us not be worried about it. A modern poet puts it very nicely when he says:-

> *'For every ailment under the sun,*
> *There is a remedy, or there is none;*
> *If there be one, try to find it,*
> *If there be none, never mind it.'*

There are many who keep their balance when everything goes well. But when disappointments come, business failure, sickness, death in the family – they lose their balance. They become elated or depressed. The wise man controls his own reactions in moments of success.

This does not mean that we should be gloomy fellows who do not laugh or smile. Far from it. When control has been acquired in times of success, it becomes possible to exercise it in times of distress as well. In times of distress one must bear in mind that he is not the only person involved. There are many others who face similar problems.

It may even be that one's troubles are nothing when compared to those of others. The fact that others are in the same position as one is may not solve problems, but one can gain a sense of relief from the fellowship in adversity.

There cannot be true happiness in a changing world. We have only to look around to be convinced of this truth. Which is the home that has not mourned the death of a near and dear one? Is there any person who is free from sickness and old age? There may be some at this moment who are free from any great trouble of both mind and body. But very soon the law of impermanence will lay its cruel hands on them. And then all youth will end in old age, all health in sickness, all strength in impotence, all beauty in ugliness, and all life in death. Nothing can stop this – not even regal power, knowledge or wealth.

What then should be our attitude to this changing world? Weeping is in vain. That will make matters worse. Understanding the true nature of the world let us face life bravely. Let us remember the advice given by the Buddha to Nakulapita. Nakulapita, in his old age, broken down and sick, visits the Buddha, and the Buddha tells him, 'Though sick of body, *mind shall be healthy.* Thus should you train yourself' Happiness is a state of the mind.

It is not what happens but our reactions to what happens that determines our degree of happiness or misery. Circumstances have the power to disrupt our peace of mind only as we let them. Events are things of the external world. Happiness belongs to the internal world. It is not what happens without but the reaction within that counts.

> *'It is easy enough to be pleasant*
> *When life flows along like a song;*
> *But the man worthwhile,*
> *Is the man who can smile*
> *When life goes dead wrong.'*

Many people have suffered from frustration and nervous breakdowns because they have not trained their minds to maintain calmness in the face of disturbances. They have only allowed their minds to develop craving to satisfy their sensual pleasures. To people who have no religious guidance, development means the increase of craving for various kinds of pleasures which are provided by the senses.

As a result people also develop very unhealthy attitudes that create jealousy, enmity, hatred which then turns into violence. That is how undisciplined people have turned the whole world into a battlefield. Once there is violence everyone cries for peace for some time. Then that episode is forgotten and a new one erupts and there is more suffering.

Not knowing that the undeveloped mind is the cause of all these problems, people accuse the devil of putting them in misery. To fight the devil they turn to god. They start to pray and worship this or that god to help them. They do all kinds of things to escape from their problems, which were mostly created by themselves. Now we can understand who creates the problems.

The Buddha says the world is within you. When you discipline yourself the whole world is disciplined and peace is maintained not only for yourself but all those around you. It is not necessary for anyone to beg the divine forces for peace. Good and bad, peace and violence do not come from outside. They all exist because of the mental attitude of people.

Spiritually immature people believe that they can find the source of their problems if they discover the origin of the world. The Buddha has advised us not to be bothered about the beginning of the world since such speculation does not contribute anything to solve our problems.

Human beings have more craving

Human beings are more selfish in their craving for pleasure than any other living beings. They enjoy the worldly life and give in to sensual pleasure with no thought for the welfare of others. Sensual people like to live long to experience more pleasures. They develop craving towards property and accumulate more property and are afraid to die because they do not want to part with their property.

Other living beings have no such selfish ideas based on collecting things and hanging on to them. They use their five senses only for their survival and lead a natural life without wilfully cheating others. It has been said that only humans hoard more than they can eat. All the other animals take only as much as they need. What they do not need they leave alone for others.

'Wealth is like sea-water; the more we drink, the thirstier we become; and the same is true of fame.'
(Arthur Schopenhauer)

Our delusion also creates problems

Actually we suffer from many of our problems because they are the result of our illusions and hallucinations. By following the Buddha's advice we can eradicate our human weaknesses. We do not use our intelligence when we come to superstitious beliefs. We must try to get rid of them by strengthening our mind and developing self-confidence. Then we can overcome many of our problems and in most cases our imaginary problems will simply disappear.

Some religions try to escape from reality by saying that god is responsible for all the good things that happened to us and if anything goes wrong then the devil is to be blamed for that. To Buddhists there is no meaning in this kind of belief.

Most of us simply do not try to understand why we are unhappy and why we are not satisfied with our life and who is responsible for this situation. Besides all the major personal problems which we are directly responsible for we also create other problems on a social level like racial, traditional, religious and economic problems which divide mankind.

Conditions which have brought about the decline of mankind are the pervasive erosion of moral standards and the degradation of people acting with polluted minds. Man is constantly making mistakes: he reaches out for wrong goals, uses wrong means, and glorifies wrong values. These will only cause him to experience more unhappiness and insecurity which inevitably culminates in guilt, worry, self-hatred, and disappointment. He seeks for remedies to the problems, of course. But he searches for the solutions from the outside, not realizing that the root and solution of every problem lies within oneself.

We must know the degree of our problems

One way to find solace for our occasional mental agony and unhappiness is to compare the degree of our own sufferings and difficulties with that experienced by others. When we are unhappy we feel that the world is against us. We think that everything around us is about to collapse and that we are the only ones going through it. We feel that the end of the road is near. However if we try to think rationally and assess our situation without bias we will try to count our blessings. We will find that we are better off than many other people. It is a good practice to keep a little book where we record the good things and the bad things that happen to us. When we compare these two lists we will find life does not always discriminate against us.

In short we tend to unnecessarily highlight our own difficulties and problems. Although many others are worse off than us, these people do not seem to worry unduly. Problems will always exist and the only thing we can do is to try to resolve them instead of worrying and adding to our mental anguish and pain.

On the contrary we must determine to resolve whatever issues or problems that we may face. We should realize that we have gone through worse situations before this and that we are preparing to face new issues. That is why we use the symbol of the wheel.

When it is moving, just as life is constantly moving, no point remains in one position for any length of time. Similarly, life's treatment of us never remains constant. Remember always 'It will pass'. Come what may, with this frame of mind we will soon regain our self-confidence and we will be able to face and resolve whatever problems that are in store for us.

We have to realise that whatever method we adapt to overcome our problems, it is impossible to gain complete satisfaction in our life until we train our mind and reduce selfishness and craving. The teaching of the Buddha gives us a very clear exposition to understand the nature of human problems and how to overcome them. The Buddha says, the world is situated in *dukkha* or conflict. Here world means all phenomena including our physical body. If the world is like this how can we expect complete satisfaction as long as we exist? So by realising this we must try to maintain some sort of satisfaction in our life to maintain peace in our mind as understanding human beings.

You create your own heaven and hell

'If you want to live in this world peacefully and happily, allow others also to live peacefully and happily, so that you can make this world something which is worthy of life.' Unless and until you adjust yourself to live according to these noble principles, you cannot expect happiness and peace in this world. You cannot expect this happiness and peace from heaven simply by praying.

If you act according to moral principles by upholding human dignity, you can create your own heaven right here in this world. You can also create the hell-fire on this earth itself if you abuse valuable human life. By not knowing how to live according to this universal cosmic law, we often stumble. If each man tries to lead a harmless and respectable life, people can enjoy real heavenly bliss better than the kind that some people hope to gain after death.

It is superfluous to create a heaven elsewhere to reward virtue, or a hell to punish vice; virtue and evil have inevitable reactions in this world itself regardless of religious faith. Compassion for all creatures is the only way to create heaven.

We can have this irresistible luminous ideal for the good of society and country by breathing tolerance and sympathy for others' progress and happiness. We have come this far as a human race because illustrious individuals have shown us the way. By leading a moral life, you help yourself and help others. It seems today man is not what he is; he is what he is not. *'This planet is the lunatic asylum in the universe where people bring forward religion, politics, traditions, customs, race, way of life and try to discriminate others and create violence.'*

Life is not free from suffering

If we contemplate deeply, we have to agree that life is indeed one of eternal suffering. Every moment we are suffering, either physically, emotionally or mentally. Can we ever find a single person in this world who is free from physical, emotional or mental pain? Even those who have attained sainthood are not free from physical pain so long as their physical bodies exist. Life and suffering are inseparable.

If anybody should ask, 'What is the most uncertain thing in this world?' – the correct answer would be 'Life is the most uncertain thing.' Everything that we do in this world is to escape or evade suffering and death. If we neglect this life for even one second, that is more than enough for us to lose our life. Most of our daily routine, such as working, eating, drinking, sleeping and walking are ways and means adopted by us to avoid suffering and death.

Although we occasionally experience some sort of momentary worldly pleasures by satisfying our desires, the very next moment these same things that gave us pleasure might turn into suffering. Therefore, the noble treasure of peace and happiness need not be in the rich man's hand but in the man who has renounced worldly pleasure.

Everything pertaining to our life is subject to change and unsatisfactoriness. That is why the Buddha has explained that as long as there is craving for worldly pleasures or desires for existence, there is no way one could escape from suffering. Desire is important for existence. When existence takes place, suffering is unavoidable.

Many contemplate seeking eternal life, and yet, ironically, many seekers of longevity find life so boring that they do not even know how to pass a single day! There is a Chinese proverb on man's insatiable desire for longevity, 'Man fools himself. He prays for a long life, and yet he fears old age.'

Apparently his intention is to remain young in order to enjoy the pleasures of life perpetually. According to the Buddha, this craving for immortality is one of the causes of selfish ideas and sufferings. If you think in this way you can console yourself: *'First we are young; then we are middle-aged; then we are old; then we are wonderful.'* (Lady Diana Cooper)

Whatever little happiness we get is secured amidst many disappointments, failures and defeats. Man cannot find a life where there are no difficulties, problems, conflicts, disappointments, and so on among thousands of other uncongenial situations. Day and night man is struggling to get rid of these unpleasant situations.

When he manages to get rid of one problem, intentionally or unintentionally he would have created himself some other problems. Where then is the end of these problems? For our own survival, we have to accept such difficulties and sufferings without complaining. There is no other alternative. Suffering will always be there! Yet suffering and unhappiness are by no means inevitable. 'Suffering,' says the Buddha, 'is a disease and can therefore be cured completely when purity or perfection of mind is attained.'

Lao Tzu, said: 'I have suffered because I have a body. If I had no physical body, how can I suffer?' 'If all the mountains were books and if all the lakes were ink and if all the trees were pens, still they would not suffice to depict all the misery in this world.' (*Jacob Boehme*)

When you look at the way people suffer in this world, you can see the real situation of worldly life. Why should they suffer in this way? And who is responsible for their sufferings? According to the Buddha, each and every person is responsible for his own sufferings. They are suffering here today because of their strong craving for existence, as craving for existence influences them to commit evil deeds. This is the main cause of suffering. It has taken more than 2500 years for many philosophers and psychologists to understand that what the Buddha said was indeed true. A poet analysed our life in the following way:

> *'To the fire flies the moth*
> *Knowing not it will die.*
> *Little fish bites the hook*
> *Knowing not of the danger.*
> *But though knowing well the danger*
> *Of these evil worldly pleasures,*
> *We still cling to them so firmly.*
> *Oh, how great is our folly!'*

Buddhism points out that the duration of life is very short and we should work mindfully, vigilantly and heedfully for our salvation.

> *'People can never really understand*
> *That we are here but for a little spell.*
> *But they who realise this truth indeed*
> *Avoid suffering and quarrels'*
> *(Theragatha)*

The world is a battlefield

The whole universe is a vast battlefield. Existence is nothing but a continuous struggle, molecules against molecules, atoms against atoms, electrons against electrons and so on and within the physical system itself it is a big battleground. The mind itself is the biggest battlefield.

The man who is not at peace with himself cannot be at peace with the world and external wars have to continue in order to hide the fact from individuals that the real war is within. The most important prayer of mankind today is for peace, but there can be no peace in this war-torn world until the conflicts of man with himself are ended. 'Having seen a football match, a small child said to the mother, those people are fighting because there is only one ball, why not we give each man one ball then they stop their fighting.'

In the eyes of the Buddha, living beings tremble like fish in a stream that is almost dry, being in the grip of craving, either leaping hither and thither, like hares caught in a snare. He saw the struggle of all against all, the senseless series of predators trying to prey upon or rob their victims in which one feeds upon another, only in order to be fed upon in return.

World history tells us that racial and colour discrimination, religious fanaticism and greed for political power and wealth have created enormous disasters, miseries and suffering in this world. They have taken a heavy toll of human lives in a cruel way. Such issues have never contributed anything towards worldly progress. People who are thirsty for power and wealth and are intoxicated with jealousy and greed always create troubles and often try to justify their cruel acts by talking nonsense in the name of religion, peace and justice. We are living in a make-believe world which appears physically united but mentally divided, and at times mentally united but physically divided. The following saying indicates how changes take place in our life:

> *'We live and work and dream,*
> *Each has his little scheme,*
> *Sometimes we laugh;*
> *Sometimes we cry.*
> *And thus the days go by.'*

Man is responsible

People always talk about the uncertainty of the world situation. Who is responsible for this unfortunate situation other than the so-called smart man? How can we expect a better and peaceful world if men behave as uncultured persons? How can we enjoy our life in this uncertain world? Scientists seek to conquer nature for their own material ends.

Religious philosophers aspire to live in harmony with nature for peace of mind and spiritual achievement. You cannot change worldly conditions according to your wishes but you can change your mind to develop contentment to find happiness. A man who is absorbed in seeking only worldly satisfaction will never reach higher knowledge, for it cannot be found without strenuous search.

Materialism degrades man to the brute state while religion elevates him into the divine or noble state. In a materialistic regime men become slaves to their senses. Naturally most people dislike to face the true facts of life. They like to lull themselves into a false sense of security by dreaming, imagination and taking the shadow for the substance. *'Naturally people believe that god cure the sicknesses but the doctor send the medical bills.'*

The Buddha's attitude to worldly powers and worldly pleasures is best described thus: 'Better than absolute sovereignty over the earth, better than going to heaven, better than even lordship over the worlds, is the fruit of a stream winner – the first stage of sainthood or perfection.' By spending his life only for worldly material progress to feed his insatiable desires it is impossible for man to see the end of unsatisfactoriness in his life. According to the Buddha, this world is based on conflict, friction or unsatisfactoriness and impermanence. Again, he says that the way to worldly gain is one thing and that to salvation is another.

Human failings

Human failings, such as ego, greed, envy, enmity and hate that prevailed from time immemorial, have remained unchanged even to the present time. The perennial problems that beset human beings are due to our inability to subdue our emotions like hatred and to replace them with love and compassion. In practically every aspect of our lives, in family circles, in society, in communal, national and even international affairs, we find the ugly word 'hatred' looming large in our vocabulary and in our dealings with one another. The father hates the child's disobedience, the child hates the parents for not providing what he considers are his essential needs. In society, a person would show hate to another person because of the feeling, rightly or wrongly, that the particular person was a stumbling block to one's aspiration and so on. In national and international relationships, one country would express hate for another country because of certain actions against it.

How we are paying the rent

We must be prepared to face difficulties and problems in our day to day life. There is no existence without problems: that is the reality. We have strong craving to enjoy the sensual pleasures of the world. While we gain temporary satisfaction from enjoying these pleasures we have to pay the price in terms of physical pain and mental agony because these things cannot last and will be taken away from us sooner or later. This can be equated to the payment of rental for the body just as we pay rent for the house occupied by us.

Think of the rental as the physical pain and mental agony and the house as our physical body occupied by us on a temporary basis.

Through our body we enjoy our sensual pleasures and we must pay for it. There is nothing free in this world. Therefore if we seriously want to eradicate or eliminate physical pain and mental agony, we should subdue the strong craving force which results from the desire for sensual pleasures. So long as we are subjected to this craving force, we are subjected to the consequences of pain and agony. So we become the slaves of our craving.

To do away with the physical pain and agony and to achieve spiritual happiness we must make our choice. We cannot have both completely, although the Buddha's teaching of the Middle Path allows us to enjoy pleasures moderately while at the same time we develop our understanding to train ourselves to eventually give them up altogether. We should not look for outside sources to blame when we come across some problems as a result of enjoying sensual pleasures.

People cannot experience worldly pleasures and attachments without paying the price in worry and misery. They must be prepared to accept the consequences if they really want to enjoy the worldly life. Those who are unaware of the consequences will be deeply disappointed. Changed circumstances due to old age and sickness could cancel out these pleasures. People who are not ready to face these problems commit suicide or end up in mental institutions. We must not label Buddhism a pessimistic religion simply because it points out these realities of life! All the Buddha's Teachings show us how to lead meaningful and happy lives by understanding our human nature and the reality of the world around us.

The losing battle

Through the advances of science and technology, man has brought the world under his sway. He believes he can turn this world into a paradise by discovering the secrets of nature and gaining mastery over it. This unquenchable thirst for domination over land, sea, air and space has made him continually search for new territories to conquer in the outside world so much so that he has neglected to understand the world within himself. All the discoveries of the external world do not bring him nearer to peace and happiness: they only succeed in making his mind more tense and discontented.

Peace and happiness can be found if we make the effort. But to do this, we must, first, learn to see things in their true perspective. The act of living is like fighting a big battle. This seems like a losing battle of trying to experience pleasure and avoiding suffering and death because all beings will ultimately suffer unsatisfactoriness and, finally, die.

In the process of that struggle, they enjoy a little bit of emotional satisfaction which are mistaken for pleasure. Most people mistake this for happiness. How can there be happiness if the mind and heart are not completely free from fear, tension or insecurity!

People indulge their senses to obtain transient physical satisfaction. This satisfaction can only too easily be turned into unhappiness the very next moment. Therefore, there doesn't seem to be complete and lasting satisfaction in the emotional and physical happiness they experience in the stream of life. It is only through training and calming of the mind that selfishness and guilt are overcome and true happiness can be experienced.

The state of unhappiness amidst phenomenal progress is illustrated by the fact that about 18.7

percent of the adults in the United States (that means more than 1 in 6) suffer from some kind of psychological problems. This is the same society that has enabled man to land on the moon and conquer space. What did man gain by landing on the moon? Did he discover anything that can help him to get rid of mental disturbances, sickness, old age and death, or even to tame his mind in order to enable him to live peacefully with others? Perhaps it is a good thing that he has not yet discovered precious metals like gold or gems like diamonds on the moon; otherwise there will probably be a bloodbath among nations in their attempt to gain dominance over the moon.

All the great religious teachers have advised mankind that true happiness is not to be achieved by seeking to possess worldly things through selfish means or by trampling down others and depriving them of their human rights, but by sharing their happiness with others and rejoicing in others' happiness. Jesus taught: *'What profit does a man show who gains the whole world and destroys himself in the process?'* (Mark 8:36). One should not acquire material things through unscrupulous and selfish means.

Simplicity and contentment are essential ingredients for happiness. According to Gandhi, *'The fewer the necessities, the greater the happiness.'* The Greek philosopher, Epicurus, once said that if you want to make a man happy, *'add not to his riches but take away from his desires.'* W. Evan Wentz had this to say: *'To have but few desires and satisfaction with simple things are a sign of a superior man.'* One cause of the problems we are now facing is man's unwillingness to share his gain or pleasure with his fellow beings. Unless man learns to share and cultivate his mind to understand things without bias and discrimination, it will be impossible for peace to reign on this earth.

Benefits of contentment

One day a King approached the Buddha and asked a question, 'When I look at your disciples I can see serenity, cheerfulness and a very radiant complexion in them. I have also heard that they take only one meal a day, but I really cannot understand how they maintain this lifestyle.' The Buddha gave a beautiful answer.

'My disciples do not regret what they might have done in the past but continue to do more and more meritorious deeds. It is not by repenting, praying and worshipping but by doing some service to others that people can overcome the mistakes that they might have done in the past. My disciples never worry about their future. They are satisfied with whatever they receive, and thereby maintain contentment.

They would never say that this or that is not enough for them. That is their way of life. Therefore they are able to maintain a state of serenity, cheerfulness and a good complexion as a result of that contentment.'

Anyone can also try to maintain this cheerfulness by being contented. Should anybody ask why we cannot be satisfied in our lives although we have more than enough things, what would be the correct answer? The correct answer to give is: 'We have no contentment.' If there is indeed contentment, we would never say that we are not satisfied with this or that. We cannot satisfy ourselves due to conflict between our insatiable selfish desire and the law of impermanence *(anicca)*.

One of the best advices given by the Buddha for us to practise as a principle is 'Contentment is the highest wealth.' A wealthy man is not necessarily a rich man. A wealthy man is in perpetual fear of his life. He is always in a state of suspicion and fear, thinking people are waiting to kidnap him. A wealthy man cannot go out without a security guard, and in spite of the many iron gates and locks in his house, he cannot sleep without fear and worry.

In comparison, a contented man is indeed a very lucky man because his mind is free from all those disturbances. He indeed is rich. What then is contentment? When a person thinks, 'this much is enough for me and for my family and I do not want anything beyond that,' then that is contentment. If everybody could think in this way, then there cannot be any problems. When we maintain this contentment, jealousy can never cloud our mind and thereby we allow others also to enjoy their lives. If there is no jealousy, anger also cannot arise. If there is no anger, there will be no violence and bloodshed and everybody can then live peacefully.

A contented life always gives one hope and confidence. This is not idealistic. For more than twenty-five centuries, men and women in the community of Buddhists monks and nuns have lived such peaceful lives. They had only four requisites: food, shelter, clothing and medicine. No one really needs anything else for survival. And many Buddhist householders too, have lived contentedly not allowing their greed to overtake their basic needs. It is surprising, how little we really need to be contented. Think about it.

Nature of the mind

Human values originate in human beings – from our own rational minds. It is for this reason that we are described as 'manussa' – 'one who has a mind to think'. The word 'man' itself is derived from the Sanskrit word 'Manas' – meaning one who has a mind to reason. Lord Buddha stated that 'Mind is the forerunner of everything in this world' – thus differentiating us who have this faculty from other living beings which do not possess the power to practise rational thought.

Other living beings such as animals, do not possess human characteristics – they are unable to use their sense of reasoning, they are unable to philosophize as humans do. Thus human beings are considered as unique in this world. Being unique, their minds must be properly trained and spiritually guided through the noble teachings of religion, so that the mind can reason and work for the good of humanity rather than causing disasters in this world. *'Speaking without thinking is shooting without aiming.'*

The preamble to the 'UNESCO' constitution contains a most significant phrase: *'Since wars begin in the minds of men, it is in the minds of men that the defence of peace must be constructed.'* In the human minds originate all the evils in this world, and it is through the proper cultivation of the mind that we can cause all the evils to be eradicated for the good of humanity.

While we are fortunate to be able to cultivate our minds to work intelligently and to serve humanity, there is an unfortunate aspect within our human character that is not found in other living beings, and that is human craftiness or cunningness. The particular trait of human craftiness or cunningness easily overshadows all other important human values. It can be said that practically all the problems, suffering and chaotic conditions prevailing in this world, are the results of human selfishness, cunningness or crookedness – a trait that is extremely difficult to eradicate.

If human beings were given complete freedom to behave according to their own desires, they may even destroy the whole world within a short spell. Through new discoveries, humans have become so dangerous that even their very existence has been called into doubt. However, religion should play an important part in diverting the human being away from these unfortunate traits of craftiness or cunningness. Religion, with its noble precepts working for the spiritual upliftment of human beings, and the eradication of all evil, should serve as a compass to guide the human mind on to the path of peace and tranquility for the good and well-being of all. Buddhism, in common with other religions, strives to eradicate all evil and works for the well-being of others.

According to the Buddha, the most valuable asset for us is our ability to cultivate and nurture our mind to achieve wisdom. This is the foundation of Buddhism. Real human values can be found amongst those who have developed their minds to the fullest extent in accordance with the Teachings of the Buddha. Unfortunately for many of us, our minds are deluded, clouded by ignorance and selfishness, even though all of us have the ability to attain the ultimate – the divine nature. Because of delusion, certain defilements such as anger, jealousy and hatred exist within us. These mental defilements act as hindrances to our enlightenment with the result that we are unable to realize the real human values inherent in us.

Lead a normal life and be happy

In explaining the teachings of the Buddha, certain people have unfortunately created a wrong impression that the Buddha had advised all His followers to give up all worldly possessions and lead an unprofitable life without the necessity of either working or earning a living and without experiencing any form of worldly pleasure. (Such a view has gained currency amongst quite a number of people who are under a complete misapprehension about the Buddha's teachings).

On the other hand we must understand that renunciation is the most important aspect to have peace of mind. But that should be done through the realization of the fleeting nature of worldly pleasures. Instead of advising His followers to lead an inactive life without doing any form of work, the Buddha, in His discourse on the 'Four Kinds of Happiness' which man can experience, clearly indicated that a man must work hard in order to acquire wealth to lead a prosperous worldly life. The method to develop human values in Buddhism is simple. One must work hard and be conscientious. One must not waste one's time unnecessarily, idling away and doing nothing. Even regarding sleep, one must be rational by keeping it to the minimum necessary for health. One should not give lame excuses that either the day is too hot or too cold for the allotted work to be done. Be constructive and conscientious in whatever you do. It was recorded that the Buddha Himself was the most energetic and active religious teacher who has ever lived in this world. During His forty-five years of noble service to mankind, it was reputed that He only slept for a period of two hours each day. He traveled all over the country advising people how to lead a noble way of life but not for converting people.

Knowing well that there are human frailties and shortcomings, the Buddha advised His followers to be careful in associating with people. One must associate with good people. Certain so-called friends are far from being friends – ever ready to cheat and swindle. A certain Western scholar once concocted a prayer: -- 'O Lord, please protect me from my friends. I know how to protect myself from my enemies.' The Buddha advised us to understand who our friends are. In associating with people, we must try to understand their character, temperament and mood. The Buddha's advice is that it is better to live alone if you cannot find a reliable friend.

Pleasure and happiness

Although many disturbances are not apparent to us, certain evil thoughts which are deeply rooted in the mind may still remain. At some moment we may be quiet and look nice because there are no disturbances to agitate us, but if some disturbances arise, we soon change our attitude and become violent and ugly. At the same time the sensual pleasure that momentarily appears in the mind we mistakenly regard as happiness. It is in fact not happiness.

Pleasure is merely emotional satisfaction. The fleeting nature of pleasure is such that it disappears at the very next moment. The seeking of pleasure must not be confused with the seeking of happiness. Pleasure is elusive, temporary, and can leave a bitter after-taste. Also, it can be costly, yet unsatisfactory. Not so happiness, which does not have to be purchased; it comes from an inner source – the mind, and it is long-lasting.

The pleasure we have at this moment sometimes creates disappointment because of the fleeting nature of the pleasure. At the same time, we cannot gain happiness by keeping mental impurities such as fear, anger, jealousy, malice and ill-will in the mind. When these are not active in the mind, then we regard the brightness that temporarily appears in the mind as happiness.

A lot of nonsense

A lot of fuss
A lot of tears
A lot of people
A lot of money -
A lot of time
And all for what?
A lot of trouble
A little body!
A blob of protein
Fast unwinding,
A little corpse
Quick decaying.
No longer is it
Dear Father, mother
Or any darling other.
In spite of this
We must have
Consolations and coffins
Processions and Tombstones

Parties and mourning
Rites and rituals
Buried or burnt
Embalmed forever,
All for these little
Bloated bodies.
Sons remember
Grandsons little,
And after them
Are the dead forgotten,
Stones and bones alone remaining.
So is this not
A lot of nonsense?
(Khantipalo)

Problems in the modern age

The modern age is marked with unprecedented transcience. Changes take place so rapidly that we have lost our sense of balance. No longer is the world in the state of calm it had been in the past. This is an age of turbulence in which the traditional societies are crumbling before the monster of modernism. The rate of change occurs at a vastly accelerated pace.

Changes that in the past would take hundreds or even thousands of years to materialize are suddenly now packed into a few years, almost like the case of a boy who suffered from progenia.

Only eleven years old, he died in March 1967 in Canada from advanced ageing. He had symptoms of senility, hardened arteries, baldness, slack and wrinkled skin – the characteristics of ninety years of ageing all packed into his eleven years of existence.

During the last 100 years, tremendous changes which started in the developed countries have swept throughout the world.

We witness worldwide population explosions; rapid rise of industrial economies and urbanization; unprecedented expansion of knowledge; rapid technological innovations; the erosion of traditional values, and the growth and disappearance of new forms and subcultures.

Changes in all these spheres have had a tremendous impact on the socio-cultural aspects of societies. Rapid change inevitably produces massive transformation of society, bringing disorganization and chaos to all levels of human experience and institutions: personal, family, social and global.

People are facing frustration, restlessness and anger not quite knowing how to deal with the heightened pace of transciency and paradoxical conduct of human affairs in the political, economic, social spheres. The deep-rooted frustration is expressed through increased violence, intolerance and drug abuse in society today. At the same time moral values have changed as a result of materialism and inclinations to sensual pleasures as well as the changing socio-economic roles of the two sexes.

There has been an increase in the rates of divorces and separations, casual extramarital affairs, and incidents of sexually transmitted diseases, all indicative that the marriage institution is on trial. There are many people who believe that marriage is now an of out of date institution which can be dispensed with.

Nations have reached the pitch of insanity, especially in the armament race of building up military hardware which endangers all forms of existence on earth. If mankind does not start learning how to live peacefully with one another and use science and technology with responsibility, it is doubtful if human civilization, as we know it, can long exist. In every country today people are trying to produce nuclear weapons for the destructive purposes. It is a big competition. They also produce biological and chemical weapons for the destruction of the human beings.

In other words, Has Mankind a Future? Very limited, if the present trend of universal degradation continues. But can Mankind have a future? 'Yes', if it reforms its ways and relearns to live in accordance with the noble, moral and spiritual standards taught by the Buddha and other religious teachers.

Just as a chain is as strong as the strength of its individual links, for there to be peace and happiness in the world, individuals comprising families, societies and ultimately the world must be at peace with itself. This is also like a pyramid, its various components within the levels must be strengthened.

In the modern age man is reaching out and seeking more and more sense stimulation. The popularity of the portable radio with or without earphones, and television is a clear indication of the present trend to seek for more and more sense stimulation. By all this we have become alienated from ourselves; we do not know our own real nature, or the real nature of our mind to be more precise.

Moreover, we go about our business in social life wearing masks appropriate for each occasion. We often do not show our true feelings of jealousy, greed, hatred, pride, or selfishness. We hide them in socially accepted ways of formalized verbal expressions such as 'congratulations', 'thank you', 'deepest sympathies'. But there are times when our negative emotions are so acute that they come into the open in the form of violence, stealing, quarreling, backbiting, and so forth. But generally we try to keep these venomous snakes of negative emotions inhibited.

Problems at the personal level

It is hardly surprising today that in the so-called highly advanced societies, in the west as well as the east, which are dominated by greed, fear, and hatred, an increasing number of people experience restlessness, frustration, jealousy, and enmity.

To many, especially the youths who are brought up in the environment of affluence and luxury, life is meaningless. In anger and out of frustration, they join movements protesting against just about everything. They challenge the conventional ways of doing things by the 'Establishment' and foster the process of bringing about the loss of moral standards, disintegration of family life, and the intrusion of psychotic cults in art, dance, and fashion.

Amidst the change and affluence, people are lonely and bored. Is it not a paradox that in the world filled with six billion inhabitants, people can still be lonely? To a certain extent, this is true. But being alone does not necessarily mean that one will feel lonely. A meditator may be alone in the forest, but he is fully occupied with the cultivation of his mind. A man can be in the middle of a big crowd, and yet be completely overcome by an intense feeling of loneliness, despite the crowd.

As one person puts it: 'When alone, I'm not lonely, since I'm free to act as I wish. It is only when I'm with others in society that I experience loneliness, feeling out of place and suspicious of the discrimination, formalities, manners and traditions which society is so full of.'

Increasingly people see their lives as being empty, filled with routine work and lacking a sense of purpose. They try to overcome their loneliness by doing outrageous things – dressing in attention-catching clothes or shocking hairdos. They gamble, get involved in petty thefts or fights – anything, just to create some excitement in their lives. But so long as they are engrossed in themselves and their insatiable desires instead of turning their efforts to the betterment of their fellowman, their loneliness will continue to remain.

Out of sheer loneliness, people turn to alcohol either as a means towards socialization or as a way to drown and wash away their loneliness. But alcohol can never wash away one's troubles: it only worsens them, like feeding more fuel to a fire.

Stress is a disease of civilization

Understanding and managing stress. Stress is a term adopted by psychology and medicine from engineering science. Simply defined, stress in engineering means force upon an area. As so many forces are working upon us in the modern age, and we find it extremely difficult to cope under so much pressure, stress is called the 'disease of civilization.' Philip Zimbardo in his *Psychology and Life* traces four interrelated levels at which we react to the pressures exerted upon us from our environment.

The four are: the emotional level, the behavioral level, the physiological level, and the cognitive level. The emotional responses to stress are sadness, depression, anger, irritation, and frustration. The behavioral responses are poor concentration, forgetfulness, poor interpersonal relations, and lowered productivity.

The physiological responses consist of bodily tensions, which may lead to headaches, backaches, stomach ulcers, high blood pressure, and even killer diseases. At the cognitive level one may lose self-esteem and self-confidence, which leads to feelings of helplessness and hopelessness. At worst such a person may even end up committing suicide.

In order to understand stress, let us consider the various environmental factors which exert pressure on modern man. In this atomic age the very survival of the species is threatened. Nuclear war threatens every single human being on earth, irrespective of whether one lives in a country with nuclear weapons or not. Population explosion threatens man with severe food shortages; at present even a large segment of human population is undernourished while still others are dying of starvation and malnutrition. Environmental pollution causes severe health hazards and mental and physical retardation. Unemployment among the skilled is a growing global problem. The pace of life has become so hectic that man is simply rushing from one task to another without any relaxation. This is really paradoxical in an age when labor-saving devices are freely available and are in use to an unprecedented degree.

Competition for educational and employment opportunities is so severe that it has contributed greatly increase the rate of suicide. Enjoyment of sense pleasures has grown so deeply that it has become like drinking salt water to quench thirst. Constant stimulation of the senses is considered a necessity today, and thus pocket radios with earphones and cosmetics are marketed everywhere. Sense stimulation goes on developing but satisfaction is never achieved. It is no wonder that man, caught up in all this, is terribly confused and frustrated, and his life is intolerably stressful. This is the situation the Buddha describes as 'tangles within and tangles without, people are enmeshed in tangles.'

Hindrances for real happiness. While the above observations were made from the point of view of modern studies and contemporary conditions, Buddhism makes similar observations from a psychological perspective. Man experiences stress and suffering because of five psychological states which envelop his whole personality.

They are called *nivarana* in the Pali language, meaning hindrances. They hinder happiness and overcloud man's vision of himself, his environment and the interaction between the two. The thicker and more strong these hindrances, the greater the stress and suffering man experiences. The thinner and more sparse these hindrances, the less his suffering with a corresponding increase in happiness.

These five hindrances are the desire for sensual pleasures, anger, indolence, worry and doubt. The Pali Canon illustrates the effect of these hindrances with the help of five similes. The mind overpowered by the desire for sense pleasures is compared to colored water which prevents a true reflection of an object on the water.

Thus a man obsessed with the desire for sense pleasures is unable to get a true perspective of either himself or other people or his environment. The mind oppressed by anger is compared to boiling water which cannot give an accurate reflection. A man overpowered by anger is unable to discern an issue properly.

When the mind is in the grip of indolence it is like moss covered water: light cannot even penetrate the water and a reflection is impossible. The lazy man does not even make an effort at correct understanding. When worried the mind is like wind-tossed turbulent water, which also fails to give a true reflection.

The worried man, forever restless, is unable to make a proper assessment of an issue. When the mind is in doubt it is compared to muddy water placed in darkness which cannot reflect an image well. Thus all the five hindrances deprive the mind of understanding and happiness and cause much stress and suffering.

Happiness through moral development. Buddhism puts forward a methodical plan of action for the gradual elimination of stress and the increase of happiness and understanding. The first step recommended in this plan is the observance of the Five Precepts comprising the abstinence from killing, stealing, illicit sex, falsehood and intoxicants. Stress is greatly enhanced by guilt, and these precepts help man to free his conscience of the sense of guilt. The *Dhammapada* says the evil-doer suffers here and hereafter; on the other hand, the man who does good deeds rejoices here and hereafter.

Buddhism firmly believes that evil increases stress while good increases happiness. In addition to the observance of the Five Precepts throughout life, Buddhism advocates the periodical observance of the Eight Precepts by laymen. These additional precepts attempt to train man for leading a simple life catering to one's needs rather than one's greed. A simple life where wants are few and are easily satisfied is highly extolled in Buddhism. It is the avaricious and the acquisitive mentality that is responsible for so much stress that we experience.

Happiness through controlling senses. The next step in the process of training is the control of the sense faculties. When our sense faculties are uncontrolled we experience severe strain. We have to first understand what is meant by being uncontrolled in the sense faculties. When a person sees a beautiful form with his eyes, he gets attracted to it; when he sees an unpleasant object, he rejects it.

Similarly with the other senses too. Thus the person who has no control over his senses is constantly attracted to and rejecting sense data, as during waking life sense data keeps penetrating his sense faculties constantly. When pulled in different directions by sense stimuli, we become confused and distressed.

Our sense faculties have different spheres of activities and different objects, and as each sense faculty is a lord in its own sphere, and as they can individually and collectively dominate man, they are called in Pali *indriyas,* meaning 'lords' or 'masters.' If we allow the sense faculties to dominate us, we get terribly confused. If we assert ourselves and control our sense faculties, we can have unalloyed pleasure, so called because this pleasure is uncontaminated by defilements. It is also called spiritual pleasure. Whereas sense pleasures increase stress, this type of spiritual pleasure reduces stressfulness and increases peace of mind and contentment.

Happiness gained through meditation. The third step in the management of stress is the cultivation of wholesome mental habits through meditation *(bhavana).* Just as we look after and nurture our body with proper food and cleanliness, the mind too needs proper nourishment and cleansing. The mind is most violent in its untrained state, but when it is tamed and made more stable it brings great happiness. Buddhism prescribes two fundamental meditative methods of mind-training called *samatha* and *vipassana,* calm and insight. The former is the method of calming the shaky mind, while the latter is the method of comprehending the true nature of bodily and mental phenomena. Both methods are extremely helpful for overcoming stress. The Buddha explains with the help of five appropriate similes how meditation reduces the psychological stress caused by the five hindrances.

The man who practices meditation gains a great sense of relief and it is this sense of unburdening oneself that the similes illustrate. They are as follows: A man who has raised capital for a business by taking a loan, prospers in business, pays off the loan and manages his day-to-day affairs with financial ease. Such a man experiences a great sense of relief. The second simile portrays a man who has suffered a great deal with a prolonged chronic illness. He gets well at long last, food becomes palatable to him and he gains physical strength. Great is the relief such a man experiences.

The third simile speaks of the relief a prisoner enjoys after being released from a long term in jail. The fourth is the slave who gains freedom from slavery. The fifth simile speaks of a well-to-do man who gets lost in a fearful desert without food. On coming to a place of safety he experiences great relief.

When the stress caused by the five hindrances is eliminated from the mind, great joy and delight arise similar to the relief enjoyed by the men described in the similes. The best and most effective way of overcoming stress is the practice of meditation or mental culture. But as a prelude to that at least the Five Precepts must be observed.

Happiness through cultivation of positive emotions. The cultivation of positive emotions such as loving-kindness *(metta)*, compassion *(karuna)*, sympathetic joy *(mudita)*, and equanimity *(upekkha)* is another means of conquering stress. Strained interpersonal relations is one of the common causes of stress in household life and in the workplace.

Loving kindness is the positive wholesome attitude one can cultivate with benefit for oneself and others in all interpersonal relationships.

Compassion is the emotion which one should cultivate to help those in distress.

Sympathetic joy is the ability to rejoice in the joy of another. It is difficult for a man of mean character to entertain this attitude as the joy of another brings jealousy to the mind of such a person. Where there is jealousy there is no unity, and where there is no unity there is no progress. The cultivation of these positive emotions stands for both material and spiritual progress.

Equanimity is the attitude to be adopted in the face of the vicissitudes of life. There are eight natural ways of the world that we have to face in life. They are gain and loss, fame and lack of fame, praise and blame, happiness and sorrow. If one trains oneself to maintain an equanimous temperament without being either elated or dejected in the face of these vicissitudes, one can avoid much stress and lead a simple life with peace and contentment.

We cannot change the world in order to give us happiness. But we can change our attitude towards the world so as to remain unaffected by the stresses exerted by events around us. Buddhism teaches the way to bring about this wholesome change of attitude.

Poor and helpless animals are being tortured or killed by the so-called civilised men in their pursuit of sport and adventure. The innocent animals are exploited to gratify and satisfy the cravings of modern society. So many have to suffer and die for the entertainment and pleasure of a few.

Coping with stress

The word stress is borrowed from physics and engineering, where it has a very precise meaning; a force of sufficient magnitude to distort or deform. In psychiatric practice however, stress involves an individuals' physical and emotional reaction to pressure from his environment and from within himself. There are two major types of stress; the stress involved in loss of a loved one, or a job, or of self-esteem that comes when a person's level of aspiration is impossibly high; and the stress involved in threats to the individual's status, goals, health and security.

Stress gets its bad name because it may become an unavoidable part of life, and cause one to be constantly agitated. When this happens, it is possible to become overloaded and suffer physically or emotionally, or both.

Stress can be caused by any number of factors, including changes, both good and bad, personal problems, physical difficulties, illnesses etc. Common sources of stress are: death of spouse or close friend, marital separation, divorce, sexual difficulties, change of residence, child leaving home, pregnancy, in-law troubles, dismissal (from work), redundancy, change in work responsibilities or working conditions and trouble with the boss.

Each period of one's life has its own set of stresses. In early life, the child has to cope with the immediate family group and the demands of school, adjusting to the personality of the teacher and to the other children can be very stressful, as can the problem of boy and girl relationships in later adolescence. Then there are the academic stresses of college years and worries over career choice.

After college, for most there are the problems of new jobs as well as of the first years of marriage. These can be quite serious and often lead to early divorce. The problems of having children bear heavily on women, while men have early career problems.

Stress can lead to disease. Some of the stress-related illnesses include peptic ulcers, migraine headaches, depression, high blood pressure, stroke and heart attacks. Continuous stress can weaken the body's immune system, and as a result the system may become less effective in battling infections. Some authorities even suggest that chronic and excessive stress may contribute to the development and progression of cancer.

In times of stress the body secretes a cascade of brain chemicals and hormones, including adrenaline and hydrocortisone, that stimulate what is known as the 'fight or flight' response. Adrenaline increases the heart rate and rate of breathing, and prepares the body to fight an external threat, or flee from it. Hydrocortisone helps to maintain its readiness for dealing with stress. Thus when we hear bad news on the phone, our immediate reaction is one triggered by adrenaline, followed by an increased secretion of hydrocortisone.

The hormones that help us to cope with stress for a short period, however, can cause health problems if we are subjected to long-term stress. Constant stress causes the body to secrete adrenaline and hydrocortisone on a continuing basis, and in time their presence in the bloodstream may be erosive. Prolonged high levels of adrenaline, for example, force the heart and lungs to work overtime and keep blood pressure above normal level. In time these changes may contribute to strokes or heart attacks.

Anxiety is the feeling of apprehension, tension or uneasiness one gets when expecting danger. We all face some anxiety in order to perform difficult tasks well, but too much can be incapacitating. Anxiety disorders constitute the most common group of mental illnesses, including the phobias, panic attacks and post-traumatic stress disorder. Many people have a simple phobia – a fear of specific objects or situations. Simple phobias are fairly common, affecting about 3% of the population.

They tend to avoid social situations lest they become humiliated or embarrassed. Insomnia, or difficulty in sleeping, is common in many people under many different circumstances. In fact more than 10% of people may have sleeping problems. If one is facing a temporary but important deadline at work or is under a lot of pressure, he may worry and therefore lose sleep. Our bodies prefer regular daytime activity, so shift workers have trouble adjusting their patterns of sleep.

The best thing one can do to cope with stress or stressful situations in daily life is perhaps obvious, but nevertheless important: eat a balanced diet, get enough sleep, exercise every day and take time to do the things you enjoy. Do not smoke or abuse alcohol or other drugs. People who are easily upset and acutely sensitive to stress can try to reduce their reactions by learning relaxation, meditation and behaviour modification techniques.

2

THE ROLE OF RELIGION

How religion can settle our problems

When people get into trouble they remember their elders or religious teachers and seek their help and sometimes even ask them to pray for them. When they are in trouble they remember religion to seek some blessing for protection and guidance. Before that they do not think it is necessary for them to know what to do or what not to do according to their culture or religion.

The upward journey in the spiritual life may be regarded by the beginner as difficult but if one makes the first step forward, employing one's energy with the little knowledge one has, then half the difficulty is overcome. We should remember that the top of Mount Everest was not reached with one step but with perseverance, surmounting enormous hardships step by step.The main purpose of a religion is to help us to follow certain noble principles to avoid many self-made problems by training our mind before they confront us and cause misery. What we are talking about here is not merely understanding things intellectually because there is so much in life which cannot be explained rationally. We need spiritual solace.

In academic knowledge there is no involvement of the personal or psychological experience. Armed with academic knowledge some people who glorify science think that they can solve all the worldly problems. Science can help to overcome problems related to our material needs and also to create more problems but it cannot help us solve our spiritual problems. There is no substitute for wise people who have experienced the world.

Think about this saying, 'when I was 18, I thought what a fool my father was, now that I am 28 I am surprised how much the old man had learned in 10 years'. It is not your father who had learned. It is you who have learned to see things in a more mature way with the wisdom of your father's eyes. More than 2500 years ago the Buddha, Confucius, Lao Tzu and many other religious teachers gave us wonderful advice. This advice can never become out of date, being based on Truth. It will remain fresh forever. It is impossible to overcome our human problems by ignoring the ancient wisdom.

At the recent WFB Conference which was held in Malaysia, our previous Prime Minister, Tun Dr. Mahathir Mohd. said, 'Science can explain what and how but science can never explain why.' Only the wisdom gained over centuries of personal experience, and contained in religious teaching can help us to understand why things happen. This wisdom leads us to develop human dignity, understanding peace and happiness.

Probably the greatest source of irritations which upsets our everyday sense of well-being is our relationships with the people around us. Everyday our emotions are tested in the way we react to people we love, people we hate and those whom we are neutral to.

All the difficult problems of life will be understood more easily if one learns Buddhism. The Buddha's approach to this subject was straight forward and scientific – hence effective and far-reaching.

'Educate men without religion and you make them but clever devils.' (Duke of Wellington)

What Buddhism requires of man

What does Buddhism require of man? A Chinese scholar once asked a monk what constituted the essence of Buddhism and the sage replied:-

> *To do good, not to do evil*
> *To purify the mind,*
> *This is the teaching of all the Buddhas.*

Naturally this scholar had expected a much more 'profound' answer, something deep and abstruse, and he remarked that even a child of three could understand that. But the sage replied that while a child of three could understand it, a man of eighty could not practice it!

The Buddha had similarly cautioned his attendant disciple, Ananda not to regard seemingly simple teachings as something easy to follow.

This is the essence of Buddhism – Man is required to follow 'simple' precepts in his search for emancipation, but the practice of these can be extremely difficult. To begin with:

- one must not take the life of any living creature knowingly;
- one must not take anything not given;
- one must guard against sexual misconduct;
- one must refrain from lying and harsh frivolous speech;
- one must not take anything (like drugs and liquor) which causes him to lose his mindfulness

These are important Buddhist principles to observe. These principles are not meant for outward show but to be simply put into practice with understanding. The central problem of the spiritual life is one of active, practical application, not a matter of intellectual knowledge.

The ultimate aim of man in Buddhism is to break finally and irrevocably the bonds that bind him to constant rebirth in the repeated birth – and – death cycle of *samsara*. He is destined to be subjected to an endless round of rebirths because in his ignorance, man conceives of an enduring entity called an 'ego' or 'self'.

Taking the illusion of an ego for real he develops selfish desires. Man is thus endlessly struggling to satisfy his cravings but he is never satisfied. It is like scratching a sore to find temporary relief, only to discover that in doing so the itch increases because the sore is being aggravated.

Is there any beginning of the world?

Some people have a very shallow concept of the world and of human existence. They do not know what constitutes this world in reality. When the Buddha said there is neither a beginning nor an end to the world system, people could not understand what he meant. This was because they could not see that the world is really within us.

If you examine the whole world and compare it with your body, you can understand that the same elements and energies and conditions co-exist this so-called world and in your body. The only difference is that you have a mind to think and comprehend the nature of existence.

The extra-ordinary mental energy that human beings experience cannot be found in other living beings. However, this mental energy must be trained and controlled. Otherwise the human mind can become the main cause for all the problems in the world. When a mind is properly trained, harmony, understanding and peace prevail. Academic or worldly knowledge without mental discipline or development is more dangerous than ignorance.

Knowledge without spiritual development can be abused for destructive purposes. Everything is subjected to the universal law of impermanence. It is the nature of all existing things. They deteriorate and disintegrate according to the same universal law. The combination of elements and energies and their existence together produce an illusion of objects, which are visible and tangible. We create the concept of solidity and permanence of them due to our delusion. The causes of their change are friction of the elements and energies. When a visible object disintegrates it is the dissolution of the elements and energies, which are compounded.

This is a natural phenomenon and every component thing is conditioned in this way. There is no reason for us to regard this situation as a creation of a divine being or that it is the result of punishment for a primordial crime. Buddhists regard this as a natural phenomenon which is the result of change and impermanence.

The unsatisfactoriness of our life begins when we cling to the idea that permanence is possible. But others explain this in terms of a Divine force which is testing human beings and calling it 'God's will.'

Unlike the teachings of science religion teaches that invisible energies can affect our lives. Cosmic forces also influence the elements and energies within and around our physical body. Some of our physical and mental problems are due to their influence. Some other unknown forces also disturb our life which primitive people regard as evil spirits.

Fear, imagination, suspicion and superstitious ideas always feed on such beliefs to disturb their minds. When the mind is disturbed, they suffer from physical problems also. However, if our minds are well-trained and developed with understanding we can prevent many of these problems. This is why the Buddha says mind is the forerunner of all good and evil states. They are mind- made.

Religious conflict

Many of our social problems are also extended into religious conflicts. In fact, religion is the cause of these conflicts. The purpose of religion is to guide mankind to develop unity and a harmonious life and to cultivate humane qualities. Today however, religion is being used to discriminate against other religions and to develop jealousy, discrimination and hostility. Actually human beings are not using religion to maintain peace but to create superiority or inferiority feelings. This hostile attitude and unhealthy religious competition have even created bloodshed in many parts of the world.

Religious leaders have been guilty of praising their own beliefs as part of their valuable religious customs and traditions, while ridiculing other religious beliefs and traditions. Some others use religions for material gain, political power, self-glorification and worldly power. Religion itself has become a big problem.

Those who use religion for worldly material gain also face fear, worry, insecurity, enmity and difficulty of maintaining their authority or power. This clearly shows that the accumulation of worldly power is not the solution to overcome human problems.

Some people concentrate only on wealth. Wealth can help only to overcome certain minor problems. Worldly happiness, sensual pleasure can be gained through wealth. Money cannot eradicate natural problems. Religious teachers, philosophers, great thinkers and rationalists pointed out the nature of human weaknesses and how to overcome them. However the ordinary people regard them as mere theories and not as solutions to their problems.

Valuable human life

Human life is valuable. It is sacred and provides us unique experiences. The Buddha says: *'Rare is birth as a human being. Hard is the life of mortals.'* Human life must be cherished and guided with care if it is not to become a curse to the whole world. We should bring peace to all by acting with love, compassion, and care so as to make life worthwhile.

We are fortunate to be born as human beings at a time of great expansion of knowledge. It is important that we use this knowledge and tap all available resources to save lives, enhance the quality of life of mankind, and contribute to human civilization rather than destroying ourselves and the environment. We should make the best use of our human potential, consistent with our paramount position on earth in the pyramid of life. Just compare ourselves with the other living beings. They may have special attributes which can sometimes far surpass what humans are capable of. Some animals possess great strength and extraordinary instinctive power no man can equal.

Some insects and animals can precognise changes in weather conditions, use their profound sense of scent for communication, transmit electrical impulses to send messages, or even just sense impending earthquakes and cyclones. Their behaviour, however, is strongly governed by instincts. Compared with human beings, their intelligence is very limited.

Yet, for all their limitations, animals lead normal lives consistent with their instincts, unlike some human beings who abuse their intelligence and degrade human dignity. These people have their minds clouded with various perverted concepts, beliefs, and imaginations, and allow themselves to be misdirected to harmful ends.

There is nobody in this world who can say that he or she is completely satisfied with his or her life. Whatever pleasure is experienced or material things are gained, in the end unsatisfactoriness will be experienced. This is only natural. The question, therefore, is not whether unsatisfactoriness should be resisted or avoided, but what a person does when things become unsatisfactory. Does he act with patience and understanding or does he instead harm himself and others? The thrust of his action is linked to the extent of his greed.

According to Gandhi: *'The world has enough for everyone's need, but not enough even for one man's greed.'* Those who are wealthy desire to become more wealthy. Those who have power would like to seize more power. Thus, the insatiable desire becomes the root of all conflicts. You may ask how are we to survive without craving? Yes, craving is indispensable for living. However, one must learn to distinguish between requiring necessities for survival and gorging one's senses for the satisfaction of pleasure. There is a subtle difference between 'needing' and 'craving'.

In living, one may struggle for one's survival as well as work to satisfy one's craving for pleasure. In the process, as a result of one's mental and moral tendencies, one may commit many mistakes which can harm oneself as well as violate the peace and happiness of others.

We must be careful about the satisfaction of our craving. People destroy themselves through overindulgence. Many wealthy people often end their lives in the same way that ants drown in a cup of honey. An inordinate drive for wealth-creation does not lead to happiness but instead becomes a source of anxiety. Being so tension-ridden, many people have forgotten the art of relaxation and cannot enjoy sound sleep without the use of tranquillisers. Prolonged mental stress can reduce their physical state to a pathetic level, making them succumb to various illnesses which can lead to untimely death.

Nature of existence

It is important for us to understand the nature of existence so that we may be able to live in harmony with universal laws that govern all phenomena and lives. People do not live up to their full human potential. They waste their human lives in search of trivial ends. There can never be peace and happiness in this world if mankind continues to act this way. Humanity must change its way of life and develop its capacity for goodness.

People are misled by ignorance. They seek to enjoy themselves by thinking since life is uncertain they may die and miss the chance of enjoyment if they do not take it while it lasts. While there is certainly nothing wrong in harmless enjoyments for a happy lay life, one should not only indulge in sensual pleasures and neglect to develop the higher qualities.

Otherwise, one will depart from this world feeling unsatisfied and frustrated. Too many people suffer in terror at the moment of death because they still have so many unsatisfied wants and desires. They believe that there is much they had to do or undo, and even during their dying moments they are filled with regret because many of their desires are still unsatisfied.

Buddhism teaches us how to maintain contentment in our daily life and overcome this fear at the moment of death. An understanding of the facts of life and worldly conditions can restrain us from pandering to our senses and maintaining superstitious beliefs. It also provides us with a clear purpose in life, without aimlessly wandering in life like the dry leaves drifting in the wind. For our lives to have a sense of perspective, it is important to understand the characteristics and nature of life. One characteristic of life is *impermanency*. No matter how perfect or strong a life, system, idea or object may seem to be, it is not secure or free from changes. Therefore, it cannot be completely satisfactory. We face the danger of changes every moment of our lives.

This impermanency is linked to *unsatisfactoriness*, which is the second characteristic of life. One of the changes we have to come to terms with is an aspect which is part and parcel of life - *Death*. We have to learn how to face death which comes to all eventually. Every moment brings us closer to the graveyard. Birth and death are really two ends of the same string. We cannot have life without having death as well. Neither can we remove death in order to maintain perpetual life. If we can understand that life and death are part of the same process, and life carries on after death, there is really nothing to fear. Guru Nanak once said: *'The world is afraid of death. To me, it brings bliss.'*

Life is not created or ready-made. It did not come into existence accidentally without causes nor did it come into being in one single glorious moment of creation. It is the effect of a multitude of causes. This life has arisen because of causes, and it will in turn create further causes that will bring forth the continuation of the life process so long as craving is not eradicated from the mind. Until the appearance of the Buddha there had been no correct method for its complete eradication. There was no explanation why life's processes flow on continuously without cessation in the wheel of existence.

The human mind is constantly creating the illusion of a permanent life. But how can life be permanent if it is housed in an impermanent physical body? In fact, what we really need to be happy about is not an immortal life, but freedom from the desire for immortality.

Life is in a constant state of flux: it is never static. Life is constantly subject to fluctuating worldly conditions which blow us to and fro, moment by moment. Once a person realizes the changing circumstances inherent in all forms of existence, he will be less frustrated when things do not develop the way he wishes them to be.

Many people believe that there is an eternal entity or substance in the human life that remains forever. In the Buddha's teaching, *anatta* or non-substantiality is the third characteristic of life.

Everything is subject to the universal law of impermanence. Therefore, Buddhism does not accommodate the belief in a permanent and indissoluble soul. The belief in a permanent soul is similar to the belief of the 'indivisible' unbreakable atom which was maintained since the time of Plato up to the 20th century when the atom was finally split. Like the concept of the so-called indivisible atom, the belief in a permanent soul is imaginary without a concrete basis.

The chemistry of life

Human life is nothing but the combination of *mind* and *matter*. The mind is comprised of four kinds of mental energies: feeling, perception, mental tendencies and consciousness. Matter on the other hand, comprises the four kinds of elements: earth (solidity), water (fluidity), fire (heat) and air (motion). Life is, therefore, a flow of mental and physical phenomena which rise and fall.

When the energies of mind and matter continue to combine and operate as a system, coupled with the cooperation of cosmic energies, there is life. If the process of combination (integration) of components that sustain life stops, life ceases. The disintegration of these energies and elements is what we call 'death', while their recombination after the occurrence of death is the phenomenon of rebirth or a start of a new life form.

The scientific explanation of living beings in terms of protein molecules, amino acids, ions, and cell activities does not clearly define what life is. According to Buddhism, birth in this present existence cannot be considered as the first beginning of a life. If we try to seek the purpose of life without understanding the true meaning of existence, it is almost too easy to arrive at materialistic and hedonistic approaches. To many people, the aim of life is to experience sensual pleasures as much as they can while they are still alive. 'Let us not be too bothered with anything,' they would say, 'since today we live, tomorrow we die and there is nothing more.'

Those who believe that life is created by a god will thank god for life. Yet, they will be troubled by problems such as, 'Why were we born into this world to suffer like this? Is it because the one who created us did this by design or is it because it is powerless to change the world for the better? Why is it that some people who are born into the world suffer much more than others? Why the glaring inequalities and what is the basis and justification for the inequalities?' To some people life is a big burden. 'Would it not be better if we were not born at all?' they ask. So, instead of looking for an eternal life, they will be longing for the end of this life.

People may have different views about life as well as its purpose. It is important for people to have worthy and meaningful goals as their purpose of life, and not selfish ones. A worthy purpose of our human life is to transform ourselves so as to realise our full potentials through the systematic cultivation and complete purification of the mind.

Through spiritual development and mental culture, we can remove all stains of selfishness and defilements from ourselves and be at peace with all forms of life and the universe. When alive the human body is the most precious and the most mysterious object in the whole world. We regard it as beautiful and spend much time, energy, and money to make it more beautiful. We regard it as an instrument for pleasure and spend nearly all our lives in seeking objects of pleasure. We assume it is a vital part of ourself. It would be useful to discuss the validity of these attitudes from the Buddhist point of view.

The human body is the most intricate machine in the world. Each human body is unique not only in appearance but also in its biochemical structure, sharpness of sense faculties, disease resistance, disease susceptibility, etc. The laws of heredity alone are incapable of offering a satisfactory explanation to this uniqueness of each individual.

The body is endowed with sense faculties which are ever in search of pleasure. The eye is in search of pleasant forms, the ear of pleasant sounds, the nose of pleasant smells, the tongue of pleasant tastes and the body of pleasant tactiles. Most of our life is spent in the pursuit of these pleasures. But it remains a fact that the body texture is such that it does not tolerate excessive pleasure.

However desirable pleasure may be, the body falls ill when overloaded with them. For instance, however palatable rich food may be, when it is taken in excess, the body becomes a victim of killer diseases. Similarly, excessive indulgence in sex causes social diseases, of which the most dreaded today is AIDS, (Acquired Immunity Deficiency Syndrome), for which a cure has not yet been found. Therefore restraint in the enjoyment of sense pleasures is the best course of conduct for those desirous of health and long life.

The Buddha argues that if the body is really ours as we assume it is, it should behave according to our wishes. It should remain young, healthy, beautiful and strong as we always wish it to be. But the body hardly behaves according to our wishes and we come to grief when it goes against our wishes and expectations. The Buddha points out that the body really does not belong to us, nor is it really our self or a part of our self. We should therefore give up craving for it, we should cease to identify ourselves with it. Giving up craving for the body results in much happiness and peace.

In order to wean ourselves from our habitual identification and ownership we have to impress the repulsive and alien nature of our bodies into our minds with deep sensitivity, so that changes take place in our attitude with regard to the body. Observation of the repulsive and misery-producing nature of our bodies repeatedly, over and over again, is one sure way of gaining the realistic perspective. This is the path leading out of misery. Far from leading to pessimism this is the only way to view ourselves objectively and realistically. It eventually leads to calmness and serenity.

Uncertainties in life

By understanding impermanence, unsatisfactoriness and non-substantiality that characterise life, the real nature of life can be understood and we can act more purposefully in life. Otherwise, we will always live in a world of make-believe, suffer undue worries, and defer the performance of our spiritual duties to some future date until it is too late. There is a parable to illustrate this point.

Once a bee settled on a lotus to gather honey. So absorbed was it in this activity that it did not realize that the lotus petals had slowly begun to close. When the bee discovered that it was trapped, it was not unduly worried. Without hesitation, it said, 'I will spend the night here and when the lotus blooms again, I will be free in the morning.' But just as it was thinking these thoughts, an elephant came along, plucked the lotus and ate it, killing the poor bee. Just like the bee, we create daydreams about our future and work towards the realization of those dreams. What we do not often realize is that life operates on principles that cannot be entirely determined by us and our efforts to realize our dreams may be terminated. This is a matter of concern especially if we put off the cultivation of our spirituality to a future date rather than striving right now.

Uncertainties and obstructions will be experienced as we work towards spiritual liberation. One day, the Buddha happened to notice a large log floating down the Ganges River. He turned to the 500 monks who were with him and compared this log to a human being in search of the final escape from the miseries of life. He said that there could be no guarantee that the log would reach the ocean. It could be caught on the bank; it could be submerged in the water; it could land on an island in the river; it could be taken away by a human being; it could become rotten; or it could sink into a whirlpool.

The Buddha said that a human being who sought to reach final deliverance was just like the log floating to the ocean. His progress towards his goal could be obstructed in many ways: he could be caught up in sensual pleasures, be attached to physical and mental processes, become proud and haughty, mingle with people who lead him astray, be born in the realm of sense pleasures, and lose his sense of moral restraint.

If one really wants to 'reach the ocean', one must steadfastly keep to the 'middle stream', that is, follow the rules of noble conduct which develop one's morality, concentration, and wisdom. Any noble human being should be able to attain salvation provided he really understands his human nature and knows in which direction his salvation lies. Hinduism also highlighted human destiny in this philosophical way:

'From darkness to light
From the unreal to the real
From death to deathlessness.'
(Upanishad)

We live in an ill-balanced world. It is not absolutely rosy, nor is it all thorny. The rose is soft, beautiful and fragrant; but the stem is full of thorns. Because of the rose, one tolerates the thorns. However, one will not disparage the rose on account of the thorns. To an optimist, this world is absolutely rosy; to a pessimist, it is absolutely thorny. But to a Realist this world is neither absolutely rosy nor absolutely thorny. It abounds with both beautiful roses and prickly thorns.

An understanding person will not be infatuated by the beauty of the rose, but will view it as it is. Knowing well the nature of the thorns, he will view them as they are and will take the precaution not to be hurt.

Like the pendulum that swings perpetually, four desirable and four undesirable conditions prevail in this world. Everyone without exception must face these conditions in the course of a lifetime. These conditions are: gain and loss, fame and ill-fame, praise and blame, happiness and sorrow. *'Don't be afraid of opposition. Remember, a kite rises against, not with, the wind.'* (Hamilton Mabie)

Gain and loss

Businessmen, as a rule, are subject to both gain and loss. It is quite natural to be happy when there is gain or profit. In itself there is nothing wrong with this. Such righteous or unrighteous profits produce a certain amount of pleasure which the average men seek. Without these pleasurable moments, however fleeting, life would not be worth living.

After all, it is what differentiates our world from hell, where there is not even a single moment of pleasure. In this competitive and chaotic world, it is right that people should enjoy some kind of happiness which gladdens their hearts. Such happiness, though material, is conducive to health and longevity.

The Buddhist attitude towards wealth is such that it has never prescribed a ceiling on income. What it has prescribed is that wealth should be acquired through righteous means and expended also in a righteous manner. Wealth earned by the sweat of one's brow without harming, deceiving or exploiting others is highly commended. It is always emphasized that wealth has only instrumental value.

It should be utilized for (a) living in comfort and making one's family, parents, dependents and friends happy, (b) insuring oneself against possible calamities through fire, water, etc., (c) performing one's duties to relatives, guests and state, and for religio-cultural activities, and (d) supporting those engaged in spiritual advancement. According to one's means, on a large or very small scale, one should try to make the best use of one's resources in the most righteous manner.

The problem arises in the case of loss especially among those with little understanding of the nature of existence. Profits are accepted smilingly, but not so the losses. The losses often lead to mental agony and even suicide when they are unbearable. It is under such adverse circumstances that one should exhibit high, moral courage and maintain a proper mental balance. All of us have ups and downs while battling with life. We should be prepared for the good as well as the bad. Then there will be less disappointment.

When something is stolen, one naturally feels sad. But by becoming sad, one is not able to retrieve the loss. One should take the loss philosophically. One should assume a generous attitude that 'his need is greater than mine'. Let him be well and happy.

During Chinese New Year once, a boy aged 11 had received many 'ang pow' (red packets containing various amounts of money) but that night thieves broke into the house and stole them all. The parents felt sad about the loss, but the boy only remarked, 'Why worry? After all the money was not ours because it had been given to us, so we really did not lose something which belonged to us.' This shows that the boy although very young was already aware that it is useless to cry over things which mean little to us.

In the time of the Buddha, a noble lady was offering food to the Venerable monks. While serving them, she received a note stating that certain misfortunes had affected her family. Without becoming upset, she calmly kept the note in her waist-pouch and served the monks as if nothing had happened. A maid who was carrying a pot of milk to offer to the monks inadvertently slipped and broke the pot of milk. Thinking that the lady would naturally feel sorry at the loss, the monks consoled her, saying that all fragile things are bound to break. The wise lady remarked, 'Bhante, what is this trivial loss? I have just received a note stating certain misfortunes have occurred in my family. I accepted that news without losing my balance so what is a 'pot' in comparison. I am serving you all despite the bad news.' Such a courageous attitude is highly commendable.

Once the Buddha went seeking alms in the village. Owing to the intervention of Mara, the Evil One, the Buddha did not obtain any food. When Mara questioned the Buddha rather sarcastically whether he was hungry or not, the Buddha solemnly explained the mental attitude of those who were free from impediments, and replied, 'Ah, happily do we live, we who have no impediments. Feeders of joy shall we be even as the gods of the Radiant Realm.'

On another occasion, the Buddha and his disciples observed the rainy period in a village at the invitation of a Brahmin who, however, completely forgot his duty to attend to the needs of the Buddha and the Sangha. Throughout a period of three months, although Venerable Moggallana volunteered to obtain food by his psychic powers, the Buddha making no complaint, was contented with the fodder of horses offered by a horse-dealer. One must try to bear losses cheerfully with manly vigour. Unexpectedly, losses appear very often in groups and not singly. One must face them with equanimity (*upekkha*) and take it as an opportunity to cultivate that sublime virtue.

Fame and ill-fame

Fame and ill-fame are another pair of inevitable worldly conditions that confront us in the course of our daily lives. Fame we welcome; ill-fame we dislike. Fame gladdens our heart; ill-fame disheartens us. We desire to become famous. We long to see our pictures in the papers. We are greatly pleased when our activities, however insignificant, are given publicity. Sometime we seek undue publicity too.

Many are anxious to see their picture in a magazine at any cost. To obtain an honour, some are prepared to offer gratification or give substantial donation to those in power. For the sake of publicity, some exhibit their generosity but they may be totally indifferent to the sufferings of the poor and the needy in the neighbourhood. These are human frailties. Most people have ulterior motives. Selfless persons who act disinterestedly are rare in this world. Most worldings have something up their sleeve. Well, who is perfectly good? How many are perfectly pure in their motives? How many are absolutely altruistic?

We need not hunt after fame. If we are worthy of fame, it will come to us unsought. The bee will be attracted to the flower, laden with honey. The flower need not invite the bee. True indeed, we feel naturally happy, and are extremely happy when our fame is spread far and wide. But we must realize that fame, honour and glory are passing phases and they soon vanish. *'Avoid popularity if you would have peace.'* (Abraham Lincoln)

How about ill-fame? It is not palatable either to the ear or mind. We are undoubtedly perturbed when unkind words of disrepute pierce our ears. The pain of mind is still greater when the so-called report is unjust and absolutely false.

Normally it takes years to erect a magnificent building. In a wink, with modern devastating weapons, it could easily be demolished. Sometimes it takes years or a lifetime to build up a good reputation. In no time, the hard-earned good name can be ruined. Nobody is exempt from the devastating remark that begins with the ill-famed 'but'. Yes, he is very good; he does this and that, but his whole good record is blackened by the so-called 'but'. You may live the life of a Buddha but you will not be exempt from criticisms, attacks and insults.

The Buddha was the most famous and yet the most maligned teacher in his time. Great men are often known; even if they are known, they are misknown. Some antagonists of the Buddha spread a rumour that a woman used to spend the night in the monastery. Having failed to convince the public in this base attempt, they spread false news that the Buddha and his disciples murdered that very woman and hid her corpse in the rubbish-heap of withered flowers within the monastery. The conspirators later admitted that they were the culprits.

When his historic mission met with success and when many sought ordination under him, his adversaries maligned him, saying that he was robbing the mothers of their sons, depriving wives of their husbands, and that he was obstructing the progress of the nation. Failing in all these attempts to ruin his noble character, his own cousin, Devadatta, a jealous disciple of his, attempted to kill him by hurling a rock from above, but was still unsuccessful. If such be the sad fate of the faultless, perfect Buddha, what can be the fate of imperfect ordinary mortals?

The higher you climb a hill, the more visible you become and appear in the eyes of others. Your back is revealed but your front is hidden. The fault-finding world exhibits your short-comings and misgivings but ignores your salient virtues. The winnowing fan thrashes the husks but retains the grains; the strainer, on the contrary, retains the gross remnants but drains out the sweet juice. The cultured take the subtle and remove the gross, the uncultured retain the gross, but remove the subtle.

When you are misrepresented, deliberately or otherwise, remember the advice of Epictetus: to think or say, '*O, by his slight acquaintance and faint knowledge of me, I am lightly criticized. But if I am better known, more serious and much greater would be the accusations against me.*'

It is needless to waste time in correcting the false reports unless circumstances necessitate a clarification. The enemy is gratified when he sees that you are hurt. That is what he actually expects.

If you are indifferent, such misrepresentations will fall on deaf ears. In hearing unjust criticism of others, we should behave like a deaf person. In speaking ill of others, we should behave like a dumb person. It is not possible to put a stop to false accusations, reports and rumours.

The world is full of thorns and pebbles. But, if we have to walk in spite of such obstacles, instead of trying to remove them, which is impossible, it is advisable to wear a pair of slippers and walk without harm. Be like a lion that trembles not at sounds. Be like the wind that does not cling to the meshes of a net. Be like a lotus that is not contaminated by the mud from which it springs. Wander alone like a rhinoceros. Being the kings of the forest, lions are fearless.

By nature they are not frightened by the roaring of other animals. In this world, we may hear adverse reports, false accusations, degrading remarks of uncurbed tongues. Like a lion, we should not even listen to them. Like a boomerang, they will end where they began. Dogs bark, but the caravans peacefully move on. *'He who makes no mistakes makes nothing. Mistakes are often the best teachers.'*

We are living in a muddy world. Numerous lotuses spring up without being contaminated by the mud, they adorn the world. Like lotuses we should try to lead a blameless, noble life disregarding the mud that may be thrown at us. We should expect mud to be thrown at us instead of roses. Then there will be no disappointments.

Though difficult, we should try to reduce attachment. Alone we come, alone we go. Non-attachment helps to calm the mind. It is rather ironical that great men have been slandered, vilified, poisoned, crucified or shot. Great Socrates was poisoned. Noble Jesus Christ was ruthlessly crucified. Mahatma Gandhi who was world famous for his piety and high spiritual attainments was shot dead, the playwright Bernard Shaw remarked, 'It seems it is dangerous to be too good.' If great people can die for what they believe, who are we to complain when our good is repaid with ingratitude?

Well, is it dangerous to be too good? Yes, during their lifetime they were criticized, attacked, and killed. After death, they were deified and honoured. Great men are indifferent to fame and ill-fame. They are not upset when they are criticized or maligned for they work not for name or fame. They are indifferent whether others recognize their services or not.

Praise and blame

Praise and blame are two more worldly conditions that affect man. It is natural to be elated when praised and to be depressed when blamed. Amidst praise and blame, the Buddha says, the wise exhibit neither elation nor depression. Like a solid rock that is not shaken by the wind they stand unmoved. Praise if worthy, is pleasing to the ears. If unworthy, as in the case of flattery, though pleasing, is deceptive. But they are all sounds which will produce no effect if they do not reach our ears.

From a worldly standpoint, a word of praise goes a long way. By praising a little, a favour can easily be obtained. One word of merited praise is sufficient to attract an audience before one speaks. If, at the outset, a speaker praises the audience, he will have an attentive ear. If he criticizes the audience at the outset, the response will not be satisfactory. The cultured do not resort to flattery; nor do they wish to be considered wrong. The praiseworthy they praise without envy. The blameworthy they censure out of compassion with the object of reforming them. *'If you have no critics you likely have no successes.'* (Malcolm Forbes)

Many who knew the Buddha intimately extolled his virtues in their own way. They sang praises of the Buddha enumerating a hundred virtues extempore. They are a subject of meditation to the devout. These well-merited virtues are still a great inspiration to his followers. How about blame?

The Buddha says: 'They who speak much are blamed. They who speak little are blamed. They who are silent are also blamed. In this world there is none who is not blamed!' Blame seems to be a universal legacy of mankind. The majority of the people in the world, remarks the Buddha, are ill-disciplined. However, just as an elephant in the battle-field endures all arrows shot at him, even so, the Buddha suffers all insults.

The deluded and the wicked are prone to seek only the ugliness in others but not the good and beautiful. None, with the single exception of a Buddha, is perfectly good. Nobody is totally bad either. There is evil in the best of us. There is good in the worst of us. One may work with pure motives. But the outside world may misconstrue his actions and impute outrageous motives. One may stretch oneself to help others by incurring debt or selling property to save a friend in trouble; but later, the deluded beneficiary may find fault with him, blackmail him, blemish his good name and will rejoice in his downfall.

In the Jataka stories, it is stated that Guttila the musician taught everything he knew to his pupil without a closed fist, but the ungrateful pupil tried unsuccessfully to compete with his teacher to ruin him. On one occasion, the Buddha was invited by a brahmin for alms to his house. As invited, the Buddha visited his house. Instead of entertaining the Buddha, he insulted the Buddha with a torrent of the filthiest words.

The Buddha politely inquired,

'Do you invite visitors to your house, good brahmin?'

'Yes,' he replied.

'What do you do when they come?'

'Oh, we prepare a sumptuous feast.'

'If they fail to turn up?'

'Why we gladly partake of it.'

'Well, good brahmin, you have invited me for alms and you have entertained me with abuse. I accept nothing. Please take it back.'

The Buddha did not retaliate, 'Retaliate not' the Buddha exhorts. 'Hatred does not cease through hatred but through love alone,' is a noble utterance of the Buddha. There was no religious teacher so highly praised or so severely criticized and blamed. Such is the fate of great men as the Buddha.

Insults are the common lot of humanity. The more you work and the greater you become, the more you are subject to insult and criticism. *'Abuse is the weapon of the vulgar'*.

Socrates was insulted by his own wife. Whenever he went out to help others, his intolerant wife used to scold him. One day as she was unwell, she failed to perform her usual unruly task. Socrates left home on that day with a sad face. His friends inquired why he was sad. He replied that his wife did not scold him on that day. 'Well, you ought to be happy for not getting that unwelcoming scolding,' remarked his friends. 'Oh no! When she scolds me, I get an opportunity to practise patience. Today I missed that opportunity. That is the reason why I am sad,' answered the philosopher. These are memorable lessons for all. When insulted, we should think we are given an opportunity to practise patience, instead of being offended.

Happiness and sorrow

Happiness and sorrow are the last pair of opposites. They are the most powerful factors that affect man. What can be borne with ease is *sukha* (happiness); what is difficult to bear is *dukkha* (sorrow). Ordinary happiness is the gratification of desires. As soon as a desire is gained then we desire something else. So insatiable are our selfish desires. The enjoyment of sensual pleasures is the highest and only happiness to an average person.

There is no doubt a momentary happiness in the anticipation, gratification and recollection of material pleasures. This kind of happiness is highly prized by the sensualist, but it is illusory and temporary. Can material possessions give one genuine happiness? If so, millionaires should not feel frustrated with life. In certain advanced countries which have reached the zenith of material progress, many people are not leading a happy life. Why should it be so if material possessions alone can give happiness?

Can dominion over the whole world produce true happiness? Alexander the Great, who triumphantly marched to India, conquering the lands on the way, sighed for a lack of more land to conquer.

When we read the pages of modern history we are appalled by the horrors inflicted by monsters like Pol Pot, Idi Amin, Hitler who massacred so many millions of innocent human beings. These people believed that they could create a new world by eliminating those who were different from them. But what did they gain? The whole world condemns and hates them.

Very often the lives of statesmen who would wield power are very unsafe. The pathetic cases of Mahatma Gandhi and John Kennedy are illustrative examples. Real happiness is found within, and is not to be defined in terms of wealth, power, honours, or conquests. If worldly possessions are forcibly or unjustly obtained, or are misdirected, or even viewed with attachment, they will be a source of pain and sorrow for the possessors.

What is happiness to one may not be happiness to another. What is meat and drink to one may be poison to another. The Buddha mentioned four kinds of happiness for a worldly life. They are the happiness of possession (*atthi sukha*) – health, wealth, longevity, beauty, joy, strength, property, children, etc. The second source of happiness is derived by the enjoyment of such possessions (*bhoga sukha*).

Ordinary men and women like enjoyment. The Buddha does not advise all to renounce their worldly pleasures and retire to solitude. The enjoyment of wealth lies not only in using it for ourselves but also in giving it for the welfare of others. What we eat is only temporary. What we preserve we leave behind when we go. What we had given we take with us. We are remembered forever by the good deeds we have done with our worldly possessions.

The Prophet Mohammad has said that the only thing which we can rightly claim as ours is what we have consumed, given away in charity and contributed to religion. Nothing else is ours.

Not falling into debt (*anana sukha*) is another source of happiness. If we are contented with what we have and if we are economical, we need not be in debt. Debtors live in mental agony and are under obligation to their creditors. Though poor, when debt free, we feel relieved and are mentally happy. Leading a blameless life (*anavajja sukha*) is one of the best sources of happiness for a layman.

A blameless person is a blessing to himself and to others. He is admired by all and feels happier, being affected by the peaceful vibrations of others. It should be stated, however, that it is very difficult to get a good name from all. Noble-minded persons are concerned only with a blameless life and are indifferent to external praise.

The majority in this world delight themselves in enjoying pleasures while some others seek delight in renunciation. Non-attachment or the transcending of material pleasures is happiness to the spiritually minded. Ordinary happiness we welcome, but not its opposite – sorrow which is rather difficult to endure. Sorrow or suffering comes in different guises. We suffer when we are subject to old age which is natural. With equanimity we have to bear the sufferings of old age. More painful than sufferings due to old age are sufferings caused by disease. Even the slightest toothache or headache is sometimes unbearable until a bigger problem strikes.

When we are subject to disease, we should learn to bear it patiently. Well, we must console ourselves thinking that we have escaped from a much more serious disease. Very often we are separated from our dear ones. Such separation causes great mental pain. We should understand that all association must end with separation. Here is a good opportunity to practise equanimity. More often than not we are compelled to put up with the unpleasant which we detest. We should be able to bear them.

Perhaps, we are reaping the effects of our own Kamma, past or present. We should try to accommodate the new situation or try to overcome the obstacles by some other means.

'Laugh, and the world laugh with you;

Weep, and you weep alone.' (Ella Wheeler Wilcox)

Even the Buddha, a perfect being, having destroyed all defilements, had to endure physical suffering caused by disease and accidents. The Buddha was constantly subjected to headache. His last illness caused him much physical suffering. As a result of Devadatta's hurling a rock to kill him, his foot was wounded by a splinter which required an operation.

At other times he was compelled to starve. Due to the disobedience of his own pupils, he was compelled to retire to a forest for three months. In a forest on a couch of leaves spread on a rough ground, enduring cold winds, he maintained perfect equanimity. Admist pain and happiness, he lived with a balanced mind.

Death is the greatest sorrow we have to face in the course of our wanderings in samsara. Sometimes, death comes in numbers which may be difficult to endure. Patacara lost her dear ones – parents, husband, brother and two children – and she went mad. The Buddha consoled her and she learnt how to cope with her suffering with understanding.

Kisa Gotami lost her only infant and she went in search of a remedy to revive him. She carried the corpse of her son; she approached the Buddha and asked for a remedy. 'Well, sister, can you bring some mustard seeds?' 'Certainly, Lord!' 'But, sister, it has to be from a family where no one has died.'

Mustard seeds she found, but not a place where death had not visited. She understood the nature of life. When a mother was questioned why she did not weep over the tragic death of her only son, she replied, 'Uninvited he came. Uninformed he went. As he came so he went. Why should we weep?

As fruits fall from a tree – tender, ripe or old – even so we die in our infancy, in the prime of life, or in old age. The sun rises in the east only to set in the west. Flowers bloom in the morning to fade in the evening. Inevitable death comes to all without exception; we have to face it with perfect equanimity.

> 'Just as the earth
> whatever is thrown upon her
> whether sweet or foul,
> Indifferent to all alike,
> Nor hatred shows, nor amity,
> So likewise he with good nor ill,
> Must even-balanced ever be.'

The Buddha says, *'When touched by worldly conditions, the mind of an Arahant (Saint) never wavers.'* Amidst gain and loss, fame and ill-fame, praise and blame, happiness and sorrow, let us try to maintain a balanced mind. The Buddha beautifully illustrates the struggle of the six senses with an eloquent simile.

According to this simile, six animals having different habits and diverse fields of action are tied together in one knot by a strong rope. The six animals are a crocodile who tries to run to the water, a bird who tries to fly in the air, a dog who tries to run to a village, a fox who tries to flee to a forest, a monkey who tries to climb to a tree, and a snake who tries to creep into a hole. These six animals are constantly struggling to reach their respective habitats and pulling the others, but no one gets anywhere. Similarly, the six senses are constantly seeking gratification in their own spheres, and the man who has no control over his sense faculties becomes terribly confused and is stuck in his misery.

Human dignity

What is the purpose of Life? This is a very common question people often ask. It is not easy to give a satisfactory answer to this apparently simple and yet complex question. Although some people have given certain answers, according to their way of thinking, it seems that they are not very satisfactory answers to the intellectuals. The reason is that they have not learned to see life objectively and in proper perspective. They have created fantasies in their own minds about life according to their understanding capacity. At the same time we also know that many religious teachers, great philosophers, well-known poets and great thinkers are also not satisfied about life.

They have all asked 'Why were we born to this world, full of suffering?' When we read their views about life, it would appear that they, too, are unable to give a clear picture of life. Some say we are the victims of a god who makes us suffer to test our loyalty to him. Some say that life is full of suffering; uncertainty and unsatisfactoriness. Others would say: 'How nice if we were never born.'

We can understand that they have seen life according to their concepts. But the ordinary man only sees life superficially and not deeply. Some people say that there is no specific purpose in life and that it can be utilized for any purpose.

On such a theory, we need to ponder wisely: to make use of life for purposes beneficial to ourselves as well as to others instead of wasting it on unnecessary things. In this manner, the purpose of life can be defined by ourselves.

If we misuse it by violating good humane qualities, by disgracing human dignity and committing immoral practices, or by giving in to our human weaknesses, it is impossible for us to achieve something worthwhile in our life.

Conversely, if we act wisely by observing universally accepted moral and ethical principles such as exercising patience, tolerance, sympathy, humility and kindness, as well as rendering service to others and training the mind to be unbiased, then we should be able to achieve something noble and beneficial to all. Those who cultivate such virtues will experience peace, happiness, calmness and satisfaction. Life would then be worth living! It would be more meaningful and beneficial to everybody. True love is undiscriminating, unattaching, and unconditional. We should share this love with all beings. This is called compassion.

Let us try to ascertain to what extent are we able to discuss human dignity from the Buddhist point of view. What humane qualities give rise to dignity and nobility? They are the moral, ethical, intellectual and spiritual norms which we uphold and treasure in our day-to-day relationships with one another. As human beings we have minds which when developed can differentiate between right and wrong, what we should be proud of and what we should be ashamed of. These are humane qualities that we humans cherish. It is in cherishing such values that we distinguish ourselves from animals.

The word 'manussa' as indicated in our religious books, describes a human being as 'one who can develop his mind.' A developed mind means that it can discern between the ethical and the unethical, moral and immoral, good and bad and right from wrong. These are attributes of human beings but not animals. Animals act by instinct. Only human beings can develop their minds or their thinking power to very high levels – capable of attaining Buddhahood.

Before the advent of world religions, human beings were guided by two valuable factors, since primitive times, to uphold human dignity. The two factors are 'Hiri' and 'Ottappa' in Pali which are translated as 'Moral Shame' and 'Moral Fear'.

These two factors, shame and fear, invariably govern all actions of man, thus differentiating the actions of human beings from that of animals. However, when human beings fail to maintain the two important factors of Shame and Fear – when they succumb to the evil effects of drugs, liquor, lust, anger, greed, envy, selfishness and hate, they lose their balance and they lose their human dignity. Without Shame and Fear, human beings are worse than animals.

Human beings have advanced very far indeed on the evolutionary ladder. They have achieved phenomenal success in science, psychology and materialism. There are now countless religious practices, customs, traditions, rites and rituals, offerings and prayers. While we pride ourselves as civilized human beings, there are some amongst us whose behaviour and attitudes are worse than animals.

A human being worthy of respect is one who has the attributes of Fear and Shame, who is kind, compassionate and sympathetic and who is afraid to harm others but is ever prepared to lend a helping hand to those in need. These are ordinary human values which we should all cherish and uphold. We should develop our humane qualities and not violate them. By being of service to others, we develop great virtues such as understanding, kindness, compassion, honesty, simplicity, gentleness, humility and contentment. We should be proud to acquire such worthy human values. 'A monk had two disciples, one is very intelligent and active, the other one is very lazy and does not know what to do and what not to do. Then the active disciple approached the teacher and said, this disciple is useless, he does not do anything and wasting his time for nothing. Why not you chase him away otherwise I'll go out. Then the teacher said if you go away there is no reason for me to be worried because where ever you go people welcome you and you know how to work with them. If I ask that innocent man to go away he will get into trouble because nobody want to welcome him and he also does not know what to do. And therefore I must have pity on him. Therefore let him stay. That is the attitude of a real teacher.'

There are certain characteristics of human nature which we have to guard and nurture carefully into useful human values. Roughly speaking, these characteristics are divided into three aspects, our *animal* nature, our *human* nature and our *divine* nature. These three characteristics influence our behaviour in varying degrees. If we give way to our *animal nature* without restraint, we will become a liability to society.

Religion is an important tool which helps us to control our animal nature. Religion, with the noble teachings of illustrious religious leaders, should serve as a guide for proper humane behaviour.

Religion also is a tool to cultivate, nurture and improve on the various aspects of our hidden *human nature*. By sustained cultivation of our human nature, we will ultimately achieve our divine goal, – our *divine nature*. By achieving the divine nature, the base emotions of greed, lust, anger, hatred, jealousy, envy and other unwelcome attributes will be eliminated, thus making the human being more noble and worthy of the highest respect.

The divine nature depends on the development of goodwill or friendliness or care for the welfare of others, compassion or kindness, sympathetic joy at others' progress and impartiality towards gain or loss and praise or blame. This is also known as the sublime state.

It is ironical that many religionists are still under the misapprehension that one can achieve one's divine goal by the simple act of praying or worshipping and the simple performance of certain rites and rituals. We have our duties and obligations to fulfill in order that we may live as real and dignified human beings.

We have to cultivate and develop our human nature in order to achieve our divine attributes. We must practise all the human values for the good and well-being of humanity. We must do all the good we can and eradicate all that is evil.

The religions of the world have been developed to guide us and show us the correct path to live in peace and harmony. All religions should provide their followers with important and suitable guidelines to enable everyone to live, eat and work together with mutual respect, understanding and dignity. As co-religionists we should all be able to live with one another without harbouring any hatred, jealousy, enmity or feelings of superiority. Buddhism gives us such guidance.

It has been clearly mentioned in the ancient philosophies that the purpose of our life is not just to maintain a selfish attitude but the noble act of being of service to others – serving humanity. Great and wise people of the world achieve satisfaction and greatness by being of service to others. Through service to others, we benefit by developing our inherent virtues. When we serve others, we serve ourselves. When we relieve others of their sufferings, we develop our own happiness and tranquility of mind.

The nature of life

'Life wastes itself while we are preparing to live,' says one learned man. 'We have to pay the price of fear and worry for creating selfish desires,' says another religious man. 'Birth of a man is the birth of sorrow. The longer he clings desperately to life the more stupid he becomes. His thirst for survival in the future makes him incapable of living in the present,' says another Chinese philosopher. 'We are the result of what we were and will be the result of what we are,' says the Buddha. When we consider all these views, we can find the clue to understand the true nature of life and its purpose.

If our purpose in life is to please only our senses, then, we must be prepared to face various problems arising therefrom. Although scientists have discovered wonderful things for man's convenience, yet they cannot fully understand the very purpose of life. Therefore another well-known scientist says:

> '*Is there a purpose in life?*
> *What is the purpose of life?*
> *What, or where, or when?*
> *Out of space came universe,*
> *Came sun, came earth, came life,*
> *Came man, and more must come,*
> *But as to purpose: whose or whence?*
> *Why, None.*'

It seems that man does not behave as a real 'man'. According to Buddhism, man is not a fixed substantive entity but an expression, existing literally only from moment to moment on the basis of energy. Human life neither appeared nor was created as an experimental guinea pig for any supernatural being. Life has its own individual identity.

We cannot understand the real nature of life due to our own ignorance and strong craving. That is why we crave to exist in spite of having to suffer in this world. Therefore it is impossible for us to discover whether or not there is any specific purpose to life in this world without proper understanding.

Life has been described as a combination of mind and matter. As a result of this combination, a being comes into existence and it goes on changing until dissolution takes place. However, dispersed mental energy and molecules once again form elements or matter and reappear in various other forms and in different spheres as life in accordance with the behaviour of one's previous life. This continuity of the life-stream goes on endlessly as long as the Karmic energy and craving for existence remains.

Sensuality and environment

The material form of a life is equated to a heap of foam, in which feeling is like a bubble, perception is described as a mirage, mental formations are like a banana tree and consciousness is just an illusion. With such an analysis of life, it is difficult to ascertain the reality or purpose of life.

This analysis of life posed a big challenge to many religious beliefs at one time because according to the Buddha there is no such thing as permanent life or entity that exists without changing and without dissolution.

Body is nothing but an abstract generalization for a constantly changing combination of chemical compositions or elements. Life is a point in an ever flowing river and contributes its part to the great stream of life. In the cosmos there are five natural laws or forces, namely *utuniyama* (lit. seasonal law), *bijaniyama* (lit.seed-law), *cittaniyama* (mental energy), *kammaniyama* (karmic energy), and *dhammaniyama* (universal law).

It is no secret that man uses his inherent powers of reason, intelligence and creativity to change his environment for his advantage. But man is not aware that the moral force he himself creates brings about corresponding changes in his environment to his weal or woe whether he likes it or not.

The scientific analysis of the universe shows that the world is nothing but an unbroken continuity of a series of movements. Einstein says: *'All matter is made of waves and we live in a world of waves.'*

'We are part of the same waves,

If a man can be aware:

of the states of his body,

of his feelings,

of the states of his mind and

of the states of mental objects,

such an awareness will lead him to discover

whether there is any purpose in life.'

Consider how some people have grown to be so attached to the physical beauty of the human body, an attraction which is being exploited on TV and cinema. Young and beautiful film stars flaunt this message all the time: so long as one is young and beautiful, one can be happy. A nice hedonistic philosophy for the young. But what happens when time catches up with the same film stars? Only a handful are prepared to 'age gracefully'.

Many others try various means to resist old age, and predictably, with little success. Because of attachment to their past fame and beauty, some have also become psychotic, resigned to living in the past and the world of make-believe rather than in the present. A piteous plight of those born beautiful who are haunted by their own beauty. Buddhism does not encourage us to develop attachment to our human body.

We should not neglect it either, but should look after it with consideration and personal cleanliness. It teaches that far beyond the care of the body is the need to purify the mind and develop human dignity. A well cared-for body is, after all, only an instrument through which we can maintain a healthy mind.

Spiritual values

Julian Huxley says: 'Life should lead to the fulfilment of innumerable possibilities - physical, mental, spiritual and so forth – what man is capable of. And humanity is capable of greater and nobler things.'

You are born into this world to do some good and not to pass your time in idleness. If you are indolent, then you are a burden to this world. You must always think of rising higher in goodness and wisdom. You will be abusing the privileges of becoming a human being if you do not prove yourself worthy of the merit which brought you here. To waste one's existence in grieving over the past, in idleness and heedlessness is to show one's unfitness for this world.

The tree of civilization has its roots deep in spiritual values which most of us have not realised. Without these roots the leaves would have withered and left the tree a lifeless stump.

The Buddha advised us not to be lazy, but to get up and do some work and try to gain some income and protect what we have earned without neglecting or wasting it. The Buddha saw worldly life in its proper perspective, without any selfish or egoistic attitude. On the other hand, the Buddha tells us that if we allow this life to go round and round in the cycle of birth and death, while suffering physically and mentally, there is no real purpose of this life. But we can make use of this life for a better purpose by being of service to others, by cultivating morality, by training the mind and living as cultured people in peace and harmony with the rest of the world. According to the Buddha, human beings are not puppets devoid of responsibilities. Man is regarded as the highest fruit of the tree of evolution.

Unsatisfactoriness

All of us experience unsatisfactoriness. How many times a day do we experience this? We can never be satisfied with whatever we gain because we want something else as soon as we get it. We want to give up something as soon as we gain it because it loses its attractiveness. We call this Impermanence.

So throughout our lives we struggle to grasp at things, and we always experience unsatisfactoriness because we ourselves and the things we grasp are constantly changing. To be really happy we must overcome this human weakness. The struggle to realize why we are unhappy, should be the aim in our life. We all like to lead very happy, contented and peaceful lives but how many of us can really experience such happiness? We are willing to do anything in everyway possible to gain satisfaction but it is very difficult to experience true satisfaction.

Suffering, in this life, comes from three main causes:

a) conflict with nature;

b) conflict with other human beings; and

c) conflict with ourselves.

A huge percentage of the suffering we experience is brought about through man's inhumanity to man. It can manifest itself as the antics of the practical joker, who under the cloak of good clean honest fun, makes the lives of his friends and family miserable. Or we find it in the surly individual who inflicts his unhappiness on others.

At the extreme end of the chain are men in conflict with men they have never known or met, raining death and destruction on a worldwide scale. Such is the nature of things. Therefore this war among humans has gone on for thousands of years and even has its counterpart in the animal kingdom.

The solution is not in reforming the world at large, but in reforming ourselves. The Dhamma will place us in a better relationship with things as they exist and will guide us along the road until suffering ceases. The Buddha has shown us that although we can help others to find the path, we cannot give salvation to others. However before we try to help others, we should help ourselves, by striving for spiritual perfection.

Immortality after death

All the questions man asks about life are related to the reality of death; he differs from all other creatures, it would seem, in being aware of his own death and in never being fully reconciled to sharing the natural fate of all other living organisms.

If only man can understand that life is short and that death is inevitable, he can solve many problems pertaining to life. In his resistance of death, man has used science to achieve some prolongation of life which may be equated to a child playing by the seaside, working desperately to build up his sandcastle before the next wave breaks over it.

Man has often made death the centre of religious objects to invoke heavenly blessings for the gaining of everlasting life.

Death happens to all living beings, but man alone has created, out of his constant fear and threat of death, a will to endure. And out of the desire for continuity in all their conceivable forms, man has created religion, which in turn, has attempted to give a more meaningful end to life.

Although certain religions believe in the existence of heavenly abodes where life would be one experience of perpetual bliss, we have yet to hear that the devout followers of any particular religion were at all keen to give up their earthly existence to be with the Almighty in heaven.

Similarly, even Buddhists would prefer to cling on to their precious earthly existence although they fully realise that life in this world is nothing but suffering, and that the ultimate bliss is liberation from suffering.

The biggest problem faced in many countries today is the problem of population explosion. Ways and means will have to be found to curb this perpetual swelling of this stream of life. These millions need food, shelter, comfort and security. To these people the question is not 'what is the purpose of life' but 'what to do with life.'

The simple answer is that one should make the best use of life and its resources and find whatever happiness that one can grasp in a practical and righteous manner rather than worrying unduly on the metaphysical proposition of the mystical purpose of life.

However, religion steps in to console man, or rather awaken him to the fact that life is not dreary and hopeless, as often viewed on the basis of the physical aspect alone. There is a hope for a better life.

All the progress in this world made by man is due to the fact that he realises he is mortal and that he would like to leave his mark behind after he is gone. If man were to achieve immortality and his days on earth were endless, he would be inclined to take things easy and lose all incentives or initiatives to progress; there would be no desire for him to make the world a better place than when he found it.

If there was no death, life would become stagnant, monotonous, unspeakably burdensome and boring. If man is given the insight to realise and know the precise time of his death, he would definitely act differently and more purposefully than what he is doing presently.

'Man's body turns to dust, but his name or influence persists.'   *(Buddha)*

Even though our ancestors are dead and gone, we can assume that they still exist amongst us, not physically, but through the influence created by them in the past from generation to generation – their influence persists.

By the term 'ancestors' we refer not only to our forebears but also to all those who had contributed for the welfare and happiness of others. In this sense, we can say that the heroes, sages, philosophers and poets of days gone by are still existing amongst us – through their influence.

As we link ourselves to these martyrs and thinkers we come to share their wisest thoughts, the noble ideals and even fascinating music they created over the centuries! The cry of a man's heart for a purpose is the dim recognition of the nature of life. When a man comprehends within himself his divine or noble nature, he no longer cries for a purpose of life, for he realizes that he is himself that very purpose. Thinking people have realized that the course of human history is determined not by what happens in the skies, but by what takes place in the hearts of men.

The Buddha said that there is no other supernatural living being higher than the perfect man. Man can and must raise himself above the limitation of his individuality, but he cannot raise himself above the laws and principal characteristics of his kind.

Why fear to depart from this world?

For most people, death is an unwelcome event. With so many cravings to be satisfied, the business of living in spite of enormous suffering is never quite finished. People feel more comfortable with the mirage of happiness than with the reality of death. If at all they have to think about it, it only has a slot in the eleventh hour.

Attachments to worldly life create a morbid fear of death. But the truth is that all life is nothing but suffering. Death is natural and inevitable. It is not half as frightening as the thought of dying itself. The mind has an ability of its own to create and to stretch wrong images of death.

The reason is that a mind untrained to see life with all its impermanence and unsatisfactoriness, is likely to cling to illusions just as a drowning man will even cling to a straw. It creates uneasiness even for those who fervently pray to an imaginary supernatural being for forgiveness and a place in heaven when life seems hopeless. Of course the fear of death is a manifestation of instinctive self-preservation. But there is a way to overcome that fear. Do some selfless service for the welfare of others to gain hope and confidence in the dying moment. Altruism purges all selfish attachments.

Purity of the mind, non attachment to worldly things, will ensure a happy parting from this world. It is the constant contemplation on death to understand the impermanence of life, and the wisdom to correct the wrong way of living, that take the fear out of death. Strengthen the mind to face facts and realities of life. Avoid unrealistic and impracticable ambitions. Develop self-confidence. Then you will be more relaxed in overcoming your difficulties in life. *'When you were born, you cried and the world rejoiced. Live your life in such a manner that when you die, the world cries and you will be released from suffering.'*

On the other hand, we must understand that the life does not die. When the physical body is not suitable to remain anymore the life departs from the body. That is called death. However that is not the end of the life. The departed life starts to build another house or body to settle in according to past good or bad karma.

Religious principles are important

As human beings, we have a responsibility to uphold certain good principles for our own benefit as well as for others. This makes good sense because when we observe the precepts, we also protect others. So long as we are not perfect, if we like to have good neighbours, we must ensure that we have a strong fence, or else it will lead to arguments, disturbances and misunderstanding.

When we erect a good fence or wall, we not only protect our house and our family, we would at the same time, protect the houses of our neighbours as well. So observing precepts is exactly like this. When we decide not to kill or harm others, then we allow others to live peacefully without fear.

That is the highest contribution that we could render to others. We should stop swindling and cheating others so that they can live peacefully without fear and suspicion. If we know how to fulfil our duties and responsibilities, we uphold our human dignity and intelligence. Naturally, by doing so, we maintain peace, harmony and calmness in our life.

But as Robert Frost says in his lovely poem 'Mending Wall', if we are good by nature and our neighbours are good by nature, then fences become redundant. Some so called primitive societies in the past did actually live such ideal lives. But as far as we are concerned especially in urban societies, we need the fences of religions to protect ourselves and others.

To do this we observe religious precepts *(sila)*. *Sila* means discipline to train the mind. We train ourselves by observing some religious principles, knowing the dangers of violating them. There is a difference between Buddhist precepts and the commandments and religious laws of other faiths. Many people follow their religious obligations due to the dread of punishment. It is quite possible that without the threat of hell-fire many people would not take their religious laws seriously.

But Buddhists follow religious principle by keeping away from bad deeds knowing they are wrong. Of course we must add a word of caution here. Just because someone calls himself 'a Buddhist' does not mean that he is automatically considered pure! A Buddhist is one who sincerely follows The Teaching of the Buddha to make him or herself a NOBLE being. This requires much honesty and effort.

Religious teachers always maintain that human happiness does not depend upon the satisfaction of physical appetites and passions, or upon the acquisition of material wealth. This fact is also clear from empirical human experience. Even if we have all the worldly pleasures, we cannot still be happy and peaceful if our minds are constantly obsessed with anxiety and hatred, arising from ignorance with regard to the true nature of existence.

Genuine happiness cannot be defined in terms of wealth, power, children, fame or inventions. These are no doubt conducive to some temporary physical comfort but not to happiness in the ultimate sense. This is particularly so when possessions are unjustly obtained or misappropriated. They become a source of pain, guilt and sorrow rather than happiness to the possessors.

Fascinating sights, enchanting music, fragrant scents, delicious tastes and tempting body contacts mislead and deceive us, only to make us slaves of worldly pleasures. While no one will deny that there is momentary happiness in the anticipation of as well as during the gratification of the senses, such pleasures are fleeting. When viewed in retrospection, a person can understand the fleeting and unsatisfactory nature of such pleasures, paving the way to a better understanding of this reality.

If material possessions are the precondition of happiness, then wealth and happiness would be synonymous.

Wealth cannot quench the burning thirst of craving. We can never be happy if we merely seek to satisfy our gross animal desires, to satisfy our need for the pleasures of food and sex. If it were so, then with the tremendous progress achieved in every field, the world could well be on the road to complete happiness. But this is obviously not the case.

Worldly desires can never be entirely satisfied because the moment we obtain something we want, we soon become dissatisfied with it and crave for something else. When the changes and decay occur in the many things we cling to, we experience unhappiness.

The enjoyment of sensual pleasure is not real happiness. True happiness can only arise from the full freedom of the mind. The source of happiness is not physical: it must be found in a mind free from mental disturbances. Worldly treasures are impermanent but transcendental treasures like confidence, morality, generosity, honesty and wisdom are imperishable. Emotional attachment, hatred and jealousy debase a person; but goodwill, sympathetic joy and an unbiased attitude will make him noble, even divine in this life itself.

Man can develop and maintain his inner peace only by turning his thoughts inwards instead of outwards. Be aware of the dangers and pitfalls of the destructive forces of greed, hatred and delusion. Learn to cultivate and sustain the benevolent forces of kindness, love and harmony. The battleground is within us, and it is within us that the greatest battle has to be fought and won. The battle is not fought with weapons, but with mental awareness of all the negative and positive forces within our minds. This awareness is the key to unlock the door from which conflict and strife as well as wholesome thoughts emerge.

The mind is the ultimate source of all happiness and misery. For there to be happiness in the world, the mind of the individual must first be at peace and happy. Individual happiness is conducive to the happiness of the society, while the happiness of society means happiness to the nation. It is on the happiness of nations that the happiness of the world is built.

From the lessons of life, it is clear that real victory is never gained by strife. Success is never achieved by conflict. Happiness is never experienced through ill-feeling. Peace is never achieved by accumulating more wealth or gaining worldly power. Peace is gained by letting go of our selfishness and helping the world with acts of love. Peace in the heart conquers all opposing forces. It also helps us maintain a healthy mind and live a rich and fulfilling life of happiness and contentment.

3

THE SELF AND FAMILY

Why we are not in good terms with our family members

Let us consider our family members. How many of them are living with cooperation, unity, love and understanding among each other? How do we relate to them? And how much do we try to avoid them? We can invite the whole world into our room through our television sets but we are not willing to invite our next door neighbour into our houses and talk to them kindly. We have no time to look at the faces of our own family members.

Instead we spend many hours to see the faces of unknown people on the television screen. Even within one family we have no time to look at each other with smiling faces although we live in the same house. How can there be unity and happiness in such families? This is the nature of our life today.

Sometimes, getting involved with people we love is the cause of great suffering. Some people completely ignore their family members after their marriage. That is not the way human beings should behave. It is the manifestation of an animal nature. We can maintain community life by assisting each other and giving moral support to those in need. In many ways we can say that animals behave in a more dignified way compared to us humans.

Although animals do not assist each other in the way humans are expected to do in families and societies, very often, they live together. Sometimes they protect their group or their young ones from their enemies. They do not destroy their own kind but human beings are doing that.

Animals do not kill a female animals after having sex with them but humans can become so cruel to do that. Dogs do not disturb female puppies but humans molest even few months old female babies. It seems that today we are not living as real human beings. We have gone very far from our natural way of life. That is why we are facing so many problems, and loneliness and insecurity.

Problems at the family level

In this age of tremendous socio-cultural changes, perhaps no institution has changed so radically as the family. In agricultural societies, families are larger than those in urban areas, because children are a cheap source of labour in the farm. The father is the breadwinner and the undisputed head of the household. Divorce is rare, for the family provides the essential economic, religious and educational functions.

In these societies, life goes on at a slower pace, and there is more space for people to move about. Therefore, there tends to be less friction. There is a greater chance for people to wander off by themselves, to commune with nature, and return to the family purged of their anger and frustration. In situations like this, there is less chance for family ties to be broken irrevocably.

As societies modernize, many of the functions of the family are shifted to other institutions. The school has taken over the educational function and the family is no longer basically an economic unit. Marital success is measured more in terms of emotional satisfaction and less in terms of economic criteria. People now marry for 'romantic love', 'companionship', and 'happiness' rather than for a satisfactory standard of living. (If a person marries for 'love', what happens to that marriage when love disappears?) Fed by TV and Hollywood movies, too many young people think that 'love' alone is enough to ensure a good marriage. Divorces happen when young people realize that marriage needs a much stronger foundation than physical love. Of course, there must be love, but more than that there must be a willingness to sacrifice, to understand and to be patient.

Divorce

In the past, a marriage was likely to end in the death of a spouse by about the time the last child was leaving home. Divorce seemed not only wrong in the eyes of society, but, to many people, it hardly seemed to be worth the trouble. With the advancement of medicine and rising living standards, however, people tend to live longer, and loneliness seems to creep into married life.

Half of all the divorces in industrial societies occur after eight years of marriage and a quarter of them after 15. Many of the divorcees remarry, not once but several times in their adult life.

The statistics are much higher for those involved in show-business. One renowned theatre actress who had been remarried more than anyone cares to count, had told the world that marriage is obsolete and that any sensible person can live and love better without it. A famous film star once proudly announced over TV that she had had fifteen husbands before an enthusiastically applauding audience.

Surely human degeneration has reached its lowest level for people to praise a woman for her unsuccessful attempts to live and build a family life with fifteen men, one after another. While people have always expected ties with their immediate family to extend throughout their lives, this expectation is by no means always fulfilled. Many people enter into matrimony knowing that the relations are likely to be short-lived. People enter into what sociologists term 'serial marriage' 'serial polygamy', since they change marriage partners like the way company cars are changed.

With the increase in divorce rates, other social problems arise. Children often are hit hardest during a marital breakup. They are often emotionally, and even psychologically, scarred by the traumatic experience of being separated from a parent. Juvenile delinquency can often be traced to an unhappy family life and childhood experience. The methods people adopt to satisfy their lack of contentment creates problems not only for themselves but others as well.

Abortion

There seems no limit to which human beings will go to satisfy their personal desires. Of late, the number of abortions in the world has reached alarming proportions. Abortion is murder, and none can say otherwise. In one magazine '*The Plain Truth*' this process is described in graphic terms. When the abortionist's instrument first touches the uterine wall, the embryo immediately recoils and the heart beat increases. The unborn responds by attempting to escape the instrument.

'The abortionist grabs an arm or leg and rips it from the baby. Blood begins oozing from the baby. Then the abortionist finds another arm or leg and tears it off. He continues until everything is severed.' 'Finally, the dead, dismembered embryo has its skull crushed. The parts are then sucked out. It's all over in 15 minutes.'

This dramatization highlights the horror of abortion which many people are unaware of. It is not a case of ejecting some foreign matter from the body: it is a plain and simple murder of a living baby-to-be.

Buddhism is not against birth control as long as the method is to prevent conception from taking place, and life has not been initiated. But once the foetus is formed, even in the most embryonic stage, life has started. Any attempt to remove it is killing. The reasons for abortion are immaterial: killing is killing whatever the motive may be.

The union of a man and a woman in the act of procreation has far more meaning than the mere satisfaction of each other's desires. It must be accompanied with responsibility. Sex is not condemned in Buddhism which accepts it as a natural human activity. But Buddhism does not encourage the mere satisfaction of passion without judicious self-restraint. No one has the right to father a child for which he is unprepared to be responsible. And no woman should bear in her womb a child for which she does not care.

Today, people avoid the responsibilities of parenthood by killing their unborn. They exchange children for material goods and the pleasure of convenience. Today, abortion *has* become a social custom – we are decadent to that extent, at least.

Child abuse

Writers in the past had sung high praises about the sanctity of motherhood. To be a mother was considered a privilege rather than a burden. And the world's literature is full of stories of mothers who sacrificed their lives for the sake of their children.

Today's materialistic world has changed all that. There is hardly a day without some report in the newspapers about children being abused or abandoned by their own mothers. Children are battered, maimed, and brutalized by parents or guardians. Even toddlers are not spared. Some of them are battered to death by their parents in fits of anger and frustration.

Sometimes a mother, out of frustration, would decide to throw her children out of the flat window or to poison them with weedkiller before committing suicide herself. This is wrong. No one has the right to kill herself, much less another, even if the motive is love. We hear of infants being abandoned by their parents and discarded at road junctions or rubbish dumps.

It may be noted that only the human species would abandon their helpless babies for selfish reasons. This deed is below what an animal would perform to its young offspring. Therefore, while we take pride in our beauty, intelligence, physical skills and technological achievements, at times we descend lower than the lowest of animals.

Problems at the social level

With the rise of industrialization comes the mass consumption society and the goading to create unsatisfied desires on a global scale. Advanced production techniques have enabled people to enjoy goods which were once reserved for the privileged class and wealthy few. Millions of dollars are spent annually to research into consumers' buying motivations so that subtle and not-so-subtle methods are incorporated into advertisements to push sales. Not only do these marketing strategists seek to identify unfulfilled needs, they also play an important part in creating new needs where previously there were none.

They use symbols and images calculated to prod the subconscious mind to create a sense of deprivation. And the consumer is told that he can only be happy if he were to possess an object or patronise a service. We see this being used extensively on TV, magazines, and the cinema screen where beautiful models are used to sell products, ranging from cosmetics and milk powder to house paints and tyres.

Youth and beauty of the human body are glorified. The advertisements suggest that you buy a brand of toothpaste not so much for cleaning your teeth, but to increase your sex appeal. Or you will attract the admiration of two young ladies by drinking a particular brand of hard liquor. Or you might have a chance of romance if you are to fly with a certain airline. (In airlines advertisements, more importance is given to airhostesses than the safety and reliability of the air travel.)

These are methods to increase the craving of modern society. The dominant message being drummed into you is: 'No matter how much you have, you still don't have enough. You cannot be contented!' These methods create a pervasive feeling of relative poverty and a sense of deprivation.

They seem to say: 'You cannot be happy if you don't have a designer watch or a sports car which brings prestige, and, perhaps, romance as well.' Completely unaware, an average person is being baited by these provocative advertisements. No matter how much he earns: $600 per month, $6,000 or $60,000, he is still 'poor' in terms of the things that can be possessed. Is it a wonder that there are as many, if not more, crimes committed today in the rich countries as there are in poor ones?

Mass stimulation

In addition, the mass media bombards the reader and listener with propaganda and messages which provoke hatred and fear for another race, culture, religion, or government. Does this not reflect the jealousy, hatred, and ignorance of society, in general, and the individual, in particular? Music, dance, and entertainment which are meant to satisfy human emotions and bring relaxation have today become drugs to create excitement and mental restlessness, arousing the animal nature in man.

The mass stimulation of craving to a heightened fever of passion in modern society has a terrifying potential of tearing apart the entire social fabric and creating chaos in its wake. The Buddha has pointed out the danger of selfish craving in one of his discourses:

'Verily, due to selfish craving, conditioned though selfish craving, impelled by selfish craving, entirely moved by selfish craving, kings fight with kings, princes with princes, priests with priests, citizens with citizens, mother quarrels with son, son with mother, father quarrels with son, son with father, and brother quarrels with sister, sister with brother, and friends quarrel with friends. Thus, given to dissension, quarreling and fighting, they fall upon one another with fists, sticks, or weapons. And thereby they suffer death or deadly pain.'

The intense state of mental unrest, caught in the vortex of greed and hatred at the societal level, manifests itself in various forms, the most alarming and terrifying being the transformation of the world into a virtual time-bomb. Today, the threat of global nuclear destruction is a real possibility. Should there be a global nuclear war, there can be no sanctuary anywhere under the sun for man to escape to. What a mess the human race has landed itself in!

Scientific advancement which has made possible the tapping of the tremendous energy within the atom has also endangered the human species. As long as man is dominated by ignorance, selfishness, injustice and other kindred evil destructive forces, no one will be safe from him.

It has been recorded that the 'blinding flash' of the first atomic bomb on Hiroshima altered the course of world history. The flash which radiated from

Hiroshima created suffering, fear, hatred and uncertainty to millions of lives all over the world. In stark contrast, the glorious light that 'flashed and radiated' with the enlightenment of the Buddha under the Bodhi tree more than 2500 years ago was also of great significance to human destiny. It illuminated the way for mankind to cross over from the world of darkness filled with greed, hatred and delusion to a world of light filled with love, kindness and happiness.

Patience and tolerance

Those who can remain cheerful during difficult times are admirable and a source of inspiration to others. They can avoid conflicts by seeing the lighter side of things. A wise man can avoid a quarrel by answering jokes and remarks directed at him with another joke. When people humiliate us we must learn how to face them gently by good humouredly neutralizing the joke.

What should you do when you lose in a game? You should not show your temper, since by doing so you will not only spoil the fun of the game but also lose your friends' respect.

Every person is responsible for making a better world by planting the seeds of patience, love and honesty deeply in the human heart. Eventually, a new era will blossom bringing benefit to his generation and the generations to come. It is a cultured person who knows how to face difficulties with sympathy and understanding. The mark of great people lies in how they face daily irritations with equanimity. Patience is bitter but its fruit is sweet.

'Laziness is often mistaken for patience.' (French proverb)

Be patient with all. Anger leads one along a blind path. While it irritates and annoys others, it also hurts oneself. Anger weakens the physical body and disturbs the mind. A harsh word, like an arrow discharged from a bow, can never by retrieved even if you would offer a thousand apologies.

Certain creatures cannot see in the day-time whilst some others are blind at night. But a man driven to great heights of hatred does not observe anything, either by day or night.

With whom and with what do you fight when you are angry? You fight with yourself, for you are the worst enemy of yourself. The mind is your best friend but it can easily become your worst enemy.

Some varieties of heart trouble, rheumatic disorders, and skin disease are traceable to chronic resentment, hatred and jealousy. Such destructive feelings poison the heart. They foster the development of latent diseases by reducing the body's natural defences against disease microbes.

Try to be good wisely

At the same time intellect alone cannot provide the solution to many of our problems. Sometimes the intellect itself can create more problems because of the egoistic attitudes in the human mind. Kindness, sympathy, patience, tolerance, honesty and generosity also cannot stop certain problems because cunning and unscrupulous people can take advantage of such good qualities. Therefore we have to maintain good qualities wisely.

There are many good people who are affected by the amount of human misery in the world. For example we can look at the enormous amount of welfare work being done by many organisations. These social welfare workers are trying to reduce human problems but their contributions can reduce only certain problems.

One way they help to settle human problems is by distributing property and revenue of the country equally among the public. It seems that their method is also not very effective to settle human problems because selfishness, cunningness and many other shortcomings can upset the situation. 'A *wise man gets more use from his enemies than a fool from his friends.'* (Baltasar Gracian)

The danger of the untrained intellect

Today we even neglect our health and succumb to indulgence of the senses to the extent that we have become slaves to self-gratification. In a sense our untrained intelligence is the cause of our problems. Human beings are the only beings on this earth who have developed their thinking powers to the extent that they can understand that one day they have to face death. That is why they, worry unnecessarily about it. Worrying about it will not make death go away. So why don't we accept it calmly?

Shakespeare made Julius Ceasar say, *'Of all the wonders that I yet have heard and seen, it seems to me most strange that men should fear, Seeing that death, a necessary end, will come when it will come.'* On the other hand there are of course some who go to the other extreme and not bother at all about the end of their life or about what happens after that. However, the majority do worry about existing problems and also worry about the next life.

All other living beings are free from that problem. Although we cannot predict what will happen to us in the future, we need not worry about it unnecessarily. Whenever certain difficulties and problems arise there are various ways and means for us to strengthen our mind to reduce our mental agony and unhappiness.

First and foremost we must try to understand the nature of the world in which we live. We must realize that we can never expect everything in this world to be perfect and to run smoothly. The world does not always work in our favour.

In fact there is no one besides ourselves who can work out our happiness and well-being. Knowing this we must take control of our lives. People always blame the world. It is not something is wrong with the world but something is wrong with us.

Fear and worry

Fear and worry are born of the imaginings of a mind that is influenced by worldly conditions. They are rooted in craving and attachment. In fact, life is like a motion picture in which everything is constantly moving and changing. Nothing in this world is permanent or still. Those who are youthful ·and strong have fear of dying young. Those who are old and suffering worry about living too long. Locked in between are those who crave for pleasure all the year round.

Joyful expectations of the pleasant seem to pass off too quickly. Fearful expectations of the unpleasant create anxieties that do not seem to go away. Such feelings are natural. Such ups and downs of life play with an illusionary self or ego like puppets on a string. But the mind is supreme unto itself. The training of the mind, otherwise known as mental culture, is the first step towards taming mental unrest. The Buddha has explained:

> 'From craving springs grief,
> from craving springs fear,
> For him who is wholly free from craving,
> there is no grief, much less fear.'

All attachments will end in sorrow. Neither tears nor long goodbyes can end the transitoriness of life. All compounded things are impermanent. Old and young suffer in this existence. No one is exempted. Many teenagers have growing pains. Being neither frogs nor tadpoles, teenagers are understandably inexperienced at building stable relationships with members of the opposite sex. They try to show off their beauty in trying to impress their opposite sex who are flattered to see themselves as sex objects. Both try to behave not as they really are but as what they think is adult. They are afraid that if they behave naturally they will be laughed at.

Behaviour like this has the potential for exploitation. There is fear of rejection as well as worry when ego is affected. Unrequited love will often 'break' many teenager hearts because they feel they have made 'fools of themselves'. Some are even driven to commit suicide. But such excitement could be avoided if life is seen as it really is. Young people must be taught the Buddhist approach to life, so that they can grow into maturity the correct way.

'*Wheresoever fear arises, it arises in the fool, not in the wise man.*' says the Buddha. Fear is nothing but fear of the mind. One's state of mind is subject to control and direction; the negative use of thought produces fear; the positive use realizes hopes and ideals. The choice rests entirely with ourselves.

Every human being has the ability to control his own mind. Nature has endowed man with absolute control over one thing, and that is thought. Everything a man creates begins in the form of a thought. Here is the key to help one understand the principle by which fear may be mastered. A noted British anatomist was once asked by a student what was the best cure for fear, and he answered: '*Try doing something for the well-being of others.*'

The student was considerably astonished by the reply, and requested further enlightenment whereupon his instructor said, '*You can't have two opposing sets of thoughts in your mind at one and the same time.*' One set of thoughts will always drive the other out. If, for instance, your mind is completely occupied with an unselfish idea to help someone else, you can't be harbouring fear at the same time.

'Worry dries up the blood sooner than age.'
'I never take a problem to bed with me at night.'
(Harry S Truman)

Fear and worry in moderation are natural instincts of self-preservation. But constant irrational fear and prolonged worry are harmful enemies to the human body. They derange the normal bodily functions. *'The fool who does not admit he is a fool is a real fool. And the fool who admits he is a fool is wise to that extent.'* (Buddha)

Control your mind

Man's mind influences his body profoundly. The mind has just as much potential to be a medication as it has to be a poison. When the mind is vicious, it can kill a being but when it is steady and diligent it can benefit others. *'It is easy to fly into a passion – anybody can do that – but to be angry with the right person to the right extent and at the right time and with the right object and in the right way – that is not easy, and it is not everyone who can do it.'* (Aristotle)

When the mind is concentrated on right thoughts, and supported by right effort and understanding, the effect it produces is immense. A mind with pure and wholesome thoughts leads to healthy relaxed living. *'He is strong who conquers others; he who conquers himself is mighty.'* (Lao Tzu)

The Buddha says: *'No enemy can harm one so much as one's own thoughts of craving, thoughts of hate, thoughts of jealousy and so on.'*

A man who does not know how to adjust his mind according to circumstances is not a real human. Turn your mind inwards, and try to find peace within yourself. It is only when the mind is controlled and properly directed that it becomes useful to its owner and society. An unruly mind is a liability both to its owner and to others. All the terrible activities in this world are the creation of men who have not learned the way of mind control.

'Below the navel there is neither religion nor truth.' (Italian proverb)

Calmness is not weakness. A calm attitude at all times shows a man of culture. It is not too hard for one to be calm when things are favourable, but to be calm when things are wrong is hard indeed.

It is this difficult quality that is worth achieving, for by exercising such calm and control, a man builds strength of character. *'An angry man is again angry with himself when he returns to reason.'* (Publilius Syrus) *'The greatest remedy for anger is delay.'* (Seneca)

Follow nature

Modern man does not follow nature because of his preoccupation with material gain and pleasure. His mental activities are so preoccupied with worldly pleasures that he neglects the needs of moral development.

This unnatural behaviour of contemporary man immediately results in a wrong world view of human life and its ultimate purpose. It is the cause of all frustration, disappointment, fear, and insecurity of our present times.

If man is cruel and wicked, lives against the laws of nature and the cosmos, his acts, words and thoughts pollute the whole atmosphere. Nature abused will not provide what man requires for his living; instead, clashes, conflicts, epidemics and natural disasters will be in store for him.

If man lives in accordance with the natural law, leads a righteous life, purifies the atmosphere through the merits of his virtues and radiates his compassionate love towards other living beings, he can bring real happiness. One who really likes peace should not violate another man's freedom. It is wrong to disturb and deceive others.

You may be a very busy person, but spend at least a few minutes a day in concentration or in reading some valuable books. This habit will relieve you of your worries and will develop your mind. Religion is for your benefit. Therefore, it is your duty to think about your religion. Spare some time to attend gatherings held in a religious atmosphere. Even a short period spent in the company of spiritually inclined people will produce good results.

Pythagoras said, 'The world is a series of changes, sometimes in your favor and sometimes against you. When you are in charge, do good; when you are overruled, bear it.' No one can genuinely flourish and grow in a healthy spiritual way by adopting an unusual method.

Happiness and materialism

The Buddha taught that all of our unhappiness results from selfish desire for more pleasure that money can buy, more power over other men, and, most important of all, to live forever, even after death! The desire for these things makes people selfish. They think only of themselves, want things only for themselves, and do not care about what happens to others. When their wishes are not fulfilled, they become restless and discontented. The only way to avoid this restlessness is to get rid of the desires that cause it. This is very difficult; but when we achieve it, we appreciate it.

Many people believe that they can solve their problems by just having money. They however fail to realise that money itself has its attendant problems. Money cannot solve all problems. Most people never think properly. All through their lives they are like race-track greyhounds running after a rabbit decoy.

When the chase ends, all excitement disappears. This is very much like the nature of sensual happiness in the wonderland of materialism. As soon as the desired object is attained, the happiness ends and new desires arise. Obtaining the object appears to be not quite as satisfying as the chase itself.

When we lose something, remember the following advice:-

'Say not that is yours and that is mine,
Just say, this came to you and that to me,
So we may not regret the fading shine,
Of all the glorious things which ceased to be.'

Wealth is not something for you to accumulate for craving's sake. It is intended for your welfare as well as that of others. Try to make the world around you a better place to live in. Use your wealth wisely to reduce the sufferings of the poor, the sick and the aged. Fulfill your duties to your people, your country and your religion.

When the time comes for you to depart from this world, imagine what peace and bliss they could bring as you recall the past good and selfless deeds you have done. To seek wealth through gambling is like expecting a passing cloud to shelter us from the sun. On the other hand, to aspire for prosperity through diligent work is as secure as building a permanent shelter against sun and rain.

'Your property will remain behind when you die. Your friends and relatives will follow you up to your grave. But only good or bad actions you have done during your life-time (Karma) will follow you beyond the grave.'

Fulfilling dreams of riches may sound magical, but fear and worry always lie in wait for such magic to wear off. A rich lifestyle brings its share of mental disturbance. With an abundance of ill-used wealth, simple things in life like friendship, trust and confidence which are taken for granted in certain circumstances become impossible to attain. When a lifestyle begins to create insecurity, it requires wisdom to put oneself on the right track again.

Riches have their trade-offs; the happiness of owning them is diminished according to the fear and worry about losing them. For our personal happiness we should acquire wealth righteously. *'Blessed are they who earn their living without harming others,'* says the Buddha. Happiness cannot be long-lived and meaningful if wealth leaves sorrow and suffering in its wake. Wealth flouted arouses envy; but wealth well-conducted gains respect.

Your wealth can only edify your house but not you. Only your own virtue can edify you. Your dress can adorn your body but not you. Only your good conduct can.

Ultimately, it is bliss to know that 'happiness is a perfume you cannot pour on others without getting a few drops on yourself'. The world may not be what you want it to be but you can tune your heart to find happiness within it. It is only when you have suffered for doing good that you can rise above others in understanding and personal happiness.

'If we want to find happiness, let us stop thinking about gratitude and ingratitude and give for the inner joy of giving. Ingratitude is natural - like weeds. Gratitude is like a rose. It has to be fed, watered, and cultivated and loved and protected.' (Dale Carnegie)

Wise persons do not harbor feelings of gain and loss. In this way, they constantly dwell in the joy of possessing great peace of mind. Man must know how to use his youth, wealth and knowledge at the proper time and place and in the proper way for his own benefit as well as for others. If he misuses his privilege, it will only cause his downfall.

'Man must be strong enough to know when he is weak, brave enough to encounter fear, proud and unbending in honest defeat, humble and gentle in victory.'

Life in the modern age has become particularly trying and problematic. Though it remains a fact that the standard of living has generally improved, man is still suffering immensely under the weight of present-day living. The physical condition of man has been reduced to such a pathetic level that he succumbs to untimely death by killer diseases such as cancer, heart failure, diabetes, etc. to an unprecedented degree.

Mentally, he is so tension-ridden that he has forgotten the art of relaxing, and he cannot even enjoy sound sleep without the aid of tranquilizers. In this set up interpersonal relations have become so brittle and vulnerable that the divorce rate has become alarmingly high, thus letting loose a whole series of other social problems such as uncared-for children, juvenile delinquency, suicide, etc. Thus life has become a problematic burden and a solution to make life more tolerable and enjoyable is a great pressing need.

> *'We live and work and dream,*
> *Each has his little scheme,*
> *Sometimes we laugh;*
> *Sometimes we cry,*
> *And thus the days go by.'*

Some people have blessings of sudden wealth through chance of inheritance. But not many are endowed with the wisdom to protect, conserve or put it to good use. Anything that is not earned through the sweat of one's brow tends to be wasted through abuse. *'A poor man can be happy; but a happy man isn't poor.'*

In this age of material pleasure, man is not much concerned with a life after death. The Buddhist axiom is that a man reaps what he sows. If one has led a useful moral life and reached old age with a sense of fulfillment, contentment and equanimity, one has no regrets. A well-spent blameless life brings, according to Buddhism, happiness beyond the grave. Such a person is said to progress from light to brighter light *(joti joti parayano,* A. II, 86).

Adjust ourselves

The Buddha explains how to prepare for a peaceful death. One has to organize one's life and cultivate an appropriate attitude for this purpose. The instructions given there are as follows:

(1) One should not be fond of a busy life involved in various activities.

(2) One should not be fond of being talkative.

(3) One should not be fond of sleeping.

(4) One should not be fond of having too many companions.

(5) One should not be fond of too much social intercourse.

(6) One should not be fond of daydreaming.

Customs and traditions are important bonds for the learning and sharing of human experience in any community. The dilemma we face in an ever changing world is whether to live with or break with the past. There will always be a 'generation gap' between the old and the young because of differing perceptions of changing circumstances and values. The old fear the young may lose their heritage and the young worry that an ancient past may become a stumbling block in modern living. Change must always be considered carefully.

Popular culture creates momentary idols and folk heroes who portray images of conflicting lifestyles. Mass media helps to reinforce this and young minds are prone to accept everything they stand for. There may be political or social messages in such movements like the Hippie or Yuppie movements but it is vital for the young to have the wisdom of the old to separate the good from the bad. Time-tested and proven good old values do not change. Values like thrift, honesty, liberality, kindness and hard work for dignified living remain fresh in any community.

In an Asian setting, marriage and funeral customs and traditions are very important. The question is whether we should spend so much money and time to carry out these customs and traditions in the modern world. Are they really necessary? There is no better advice than what the Buddha gave in the Kalama Sutta:

'When you know in yourselves, these ideas are unprofitable, liable to censure, condemned by the wise, being adopted and put into effect, they lead to harm and suffering, then you should abandon them .... When you know yourselves, these things are wholesome, blameless, commended by the wise, being adopted and put into effect they lead to welfare and happiness' then you should practise them and abide in them.'

Every man is a creature of the universe. So long as man is concerned with humanising society and the re-ordering of the world for the better, time will always bridge the gap between the young and the old. Worry and fear over the direction of change will lose their grip.

The old only have to remember how their own parents had objected to certain modern ways of living prevalent at the time when they were young. Tolerance for differences on an issue is a virtue. An open attitude can only be a happy one. *'Love your enemies, for they tell you your faults.'* (Benjamin Franklin)

There was a headman in a certain village who had a hot tempered father. Each time the elderly man lost his temper, he would storm out of his house and scold his son. Although his temper was well known in the village, this outburst caused some embarrassment and often disturbed others' minds.

One day, the headman hung an iron ring outside his house and instructed the village boys to strike it repeatedly each time his father scolded him. The loud clanging noise drew a lot of attention, and soon the elderly man realised that he was making a fool of himself and stopped scolding his son.

Returning good for evil

If you want to be rid of your enemies, you must first kill the greatest enemy within you - your anger. If you are to be perturbed by distractions from your enemies, it means you are fulfilling the wishes of your enemies by unknowingly entering their trap. You should not think that you can only learn from those who praise you, help you, and associate with you very closely.

You could learn many things from your enemies. You should not think they are entirely wrong just because they happen to be your enemies. They may also possess certain good qualities. *'Lend to an enemy, and you'll gain him; to a friend, and you'll lose him.'*

You cannot get rid of your enemies by returning evil for evil; that will only be inviting more enemies. The best method to counter your enemies is to radiate your compassionate love towards them. You may think that this is impossible or something nonsensical. But this is the proven way of every cultured man.

When you come to know that there is someone who is very angry with you, you should first try to find out the main cause. If it is due to your mistake, you should admit it and not hesitate to apologise to him. If it is due to certain misunderstandings between you both, you must enlighten him with a heart to heart talk. If it is due to jealousy, try radiating your compassionate love. You could influence him by your mental vibrations.

You may not be able to understand how it works but the experience of many people has shown that it is the most powerful, intelligent and easy method to win friends. It is highly recommended in Buddhism. Of course, to do this, you must have confidence and patience in yourself. By doing this, you will be able to make your enemy understand that he is in the wrong. Besides, you have also benefited in various ways for not accommodating enmity in your mind.

'Do not give to others what you yourself do not like.'

Be unbiased

You should not come to any hasty decision regarding any matter when you are in a bad mood or under provocation. Any decision or conclusion reached during such a period would be a matter you can regret one day. Allow your mind to calm down first and think. Then, your judgment will be an unbiased one. Cultivate tolerance, for tolerance helps you to sympathise with other people's troubles. Avoid unnecessary criticism. Try to realize that even the finest human being is not infallible. The weakness you find in your neighbour can be found in yourself. It has been said that you should not throw stones at others while staying in a glass house. Humility is the wise man's measure for knowing the difference between what is and what is yet to be.

'The Buddha himself started His ministry by discarding all His princely pride in an act of self-humiliation. He gained enlightenment during His life, but never lost His naturalness, never assumed superior airs. His parables were not for great show. He had time for the most humble of men. He never lost His sense of humour.'

To waste a man's existence in worrying about the future, grieving over the past, or in idleness or heedlessness, is to show his unfitness for the noble place he holds as the best of earthly creatures. He will thus create bad mental attitudes which will relegate him to a place befitting his unworthiness. Bear this in mind, and do good while life lasts. By wasting your time, you injure not only yourself but also others, for your time is as much other's as it is yours.

As long as there is one single fellow creature whom you can console by your kind words, whom you can enliven and cheer by your presence, whom you can help with your worldly possessions, however little that charity may be, you are a precious possession to the human race.

You should never be disheartened or depressed. There may be times when those you love do not seem to care for you, and you are apt to have a heavy heart. But there is no just cause for dejection. What does anything matter so long as you know that you are full of compassion for your fellow men? One should never depend on others for one's happiness.

Married life

In a true marriage, a man and a woman think more of the partnership than they do of themselves. A feeling of security and contentment comes from mutual efforts. Impatience and misunderstanding are responsible for most family problems.

'An archaeologist is the best husband a woman can have. The older she gets, the more interested he is in her.' (Agatha Christie)

A wife is not her husband's servant. She deserves respect as an equal. Though a husband has the bread winner's duties, helping out with household chores does not demean a husband's masculinity. At the same time, a nagging and grumpy wife is not going to make up for shortages in the home. Neither will her suspicion of her husband help to make a happy marriage.

'If you want your wife to listen to you, talk to another woman.' If her husband has shortcomings, only tolerance and kind words will get him to see light. Right understanding and moral conduct are the practical side of wisdom.

'Women fall in love through their ears and men through their eyes.' (Woodrow Wyatt)

Marriage is a blessing but many people turn their married lives into a curse. Poverty is not the main cause of an unhappy married life. Both husband and wife must learn to share the pleasure and pain of everything in their daily lives.

'Women are never stronger than when they arm themselves with their weaknesses.' (Madame du Deffand)

Mutual understanding is the secret of a happy family life. The intrinsic characteristic of a person is difficult to change simply by accusing or blaming.

'A poor man who marries a wealthy woman gets a ruler and not a wife.' Husband and wife who have different characters, can live together through understanding their differences and acting wisely.

'Marriage is neither heaven nor hell; it is simply purgatory.' (Abraham Lincoln)

Time will heal our wounds

Trouble passes. What has caused you to burst into tears will soon be forgotten. You may remember that you cried but not why you did so! As we grow up and go through life, we are often surprised at how we lie awake at night brooding over something that has upset us during the day, or how we nurse resentment against someone by letting the same thoughts run through our minds concerning how to have our own back.

We may lose our temper over something, and later wonder what it was we were so angry about, and be surprised to realise what a waste of time and energy it had all been. We have deliberately gone on being unhappy when we could have stopped being so and started thinking about something else more wholesome.

Whatever our troubles are, and however miserable they made us, time will heal our wounds. But surely there must be something we can do to prevent ourselves from being hurt in the first place. Why should we allow our troubles to drain away our energy and make us unhappy? It is we who make ourselves unhappy, not others.

You may have some troubles in your work place but you should not infect your home with a bad atmosphere. You should realise that there is an end to those problems. The solutions could be found in achieving freedom from our selfish desires by eradicating all forms of egoism and ignorance.

Whenever we fail to find a solution to a problem, we are inclined to find a scapegoat to vent our frustration. We are not prepared to admit our own shortcomings. It is easier to put the blame on others. In fact, some even take pleasure in doing so. This is a completely wrong attitude to adopt. We must not show resentment towards others. We should do our utmost, pains-takingly and calmly, to resolve our own problems. We must be prepared to face up to any difficulties that we encounter.

The secret of happy successful living is to do what needs to be done now, and not worry about the past or the future. We cannot reshape the past nor can we anticipate everything in the future. There is but one moment of time over which we have some conscious control and that is the present.

Many people just worry about their future. They have to learn to adjust themselves to the circumstances. Whatever castles they may build in the air, whatever dreams they may have, they must always remember that they are living in this world of constant friction and change.

> *'There are no stars that we can depend on,*
> *There is no guiding light,*
> *And we know that we must,*
> *BE GOOD, BE JUST, BE RIGHT.'*

Healthy atmosphere

There are many ways of correcting a person when he is wrong. By criticising or blaming him in public, you will be humiliating him but not correcting him. Criticism is certain to make more enemies. If you can show concern for a man's future good with kind words, he will thank you for it someday.

Never use harsh or unpleasant words whenever you express your views on issues. Diplomacy, gentleness and politeness do not hurt anybody. In fact they will open many doors to relieve the situation.

Do not feel defensive when your own faults are pointed out. Your faults are your signposts for learning perfection. Temper is a poor camouflage for shortcomings. When someone loses his temper he will blurt out too many things better left unsaid. Never reveal a former friend's personal secret no matter how angry you are with him now. You will only degrade yourself in the process and others could never accept you as a sincere friend thereafter. Others will think you could do the same thing you did to injure a former friend: no one will trust you.

Sweetness creates sickness, bitterness comes with the cure. Praise is sweetness, an excess of which causes sickness; and criticism is like a bitter pill which can cure our sicknesses. We must have the courage to tolerate criticism and not be afraid of it.

> *'The ugliness we see in others*
> *Is a reflection of our own nature.'*

A man's life, circumstances and world are a reflection of his own thoughts and beliefs. All men are mirrors to themselves, sores, ills, and all. Physical ugliness is no handicap to a charming personality. If an ugly person cultivates the virtue of compassionate love, that love will show in so many winning ways - serenity, radiance, kindliness and gentleness. That kind of attractiveness will easily compensate for any shortcomings in appearance. By comparison, a handsome person with airs or pride, will look so unappealing and repulsive. Inner charm is the real beauty. It has a special quality and attractiveness.

Knowledge and wisdom

Wisdom is not knowledge. We do gain knowledge after listening, reading and observing many things in this world but it is not wisdom in the real sense. Wisdom only appears in the mind when mental hindrances, obstructions and other impurities are not active in the mind.

There are many learned people all over the world who no doubt have wonderful knowledge but unfortunately lack proper wisdom. Many people are intelligent but their behaviour however is not reasonable, as some are hot-tempered, egoistic, emotional, jealous, greedy and temperamental. Intellectuals are more cunning rather than wise.

On the other hand, there are others who are very kind and although they have patience, tolerance and many other good qualities, their wisdom is very poor as they can be easily misled by others. If we develop our generosity without proper understanding, we could get into trouble as certain people can take undue advantage of us. Understanding and good qualities must therefore go together.

'A learned fool is more foolish than an ignorant fool.'
(Moliere)

Modern education

Modern scientific education has created more problems rather than promoting knowledge, peace, happiness and security. Governments are trying to maintain peace and order by punishing those who disobey the existing law of the country. But all over the world evil and immoral practices are spreading rapidly because we cannot eradicate wrong-doing by creating fear.

If a government declared that the law enforced by the government is withdrawn, we can see how people will destroy the whole country within 24 hours. Evil people use violence and bloodshed to gain what they need and to settle their problems. Not even religious leaders are free from blame in this problem. They use other means to keep their believers fooled.

They try to make people accept their sufferings by illustrating the concept of a paradise to create temptation. They frighten people by threatening them with hell fire to do good and not to do bad things. Whatever method people adopt to avoid those problems, they experience more and more new problems. The reason why problems cannot be solved in this way is that people do not realize the root cause of most of their shortcomings. The cause is nothing but an untrained or uncultured mind.

When we study the lives of less 'developed' people we can understand that they have to face relatively few problems at least on a psychological level. Their problems are mostly related only to their needs for survival and physical problems like hunger and disease. But in the so-called civilised society of today many of our problems do not arise from our need to ensure survival. People in these societies are quite assured of material things like food and shelter, but they are still unhappy, perhaps more unhappy than the so-called primitive people.

Their problems lie in the fact that they seek too much enjoyment and do not know the meaning of contentment. Many people believe that the purpose of their life is only to seek enjoyment to satisfy the craving caused by the five senses. The modern-job orientated education system produces students who are equipped with mere factual knowledge to 'succeed' in life.

It develops selfishness because they are taught that material success means getting ahead of others. It produces clever people without any moral development. Such people do not care what happens to others as long as they can gain profit and fame on the materialistic level. They achieve their selfish desire, through cunning or cruelty, by adapting modern techniques.

The blossom time in life takes place during the transitional stages of development of the child towards adolescence. It is during their formative age that the youth cultivate the qualities of manhood. This period helps the youth to experience the varying spheres of their evolution both physically and mentally. It is during this time that the State, Home and Religion get mixed up a great deal in the common anxious effort to create the best environment for them to bring about the maximum results within this minimum period.

How to face our problems

Those who cannot cope with their problems create more worries. When misunderstanding occurs in their family they make life more miserable. Sometimes violence, bloodshed and suicide can also take place. So where is the satisfaction in a worldly life?

Today people need more income not only for their daily living such as to provide their food, clothing, medicine, shelter and to fulfill their obligations but also they have organized a way of life such that their sensual indulgence has increased. It has become a sort of competition.

People concentrate more on pleasure rather than their duties and responsibilities. Some people continue to feed their dissatisfaction by worrying about their future although they have more than enough at the moment. They worry about their sickness, old age, death and also about heaven and hell in the next birth.

Everyday they experience unsatisfactoriness in their life. They run here and there searching for a remedy to end their problems throughout their life. They continue this search for peace and happiness until they die but they never find the real solution. When they feel that they are getting old they worry, they worry when they cannot get what they want, they worry when they lose their things or person they love. This leads to frustration and mental agony and may even later lead to mental derangement. We do not know the real nature of our existence but try to maintain life without experiencing any disturbances and changes.

Life is changing, it is a bundle of elements and energies which are always changing. As a result no situation will ever be according to our expectation and we feel life does not work in our favor. When the elements and energies are imbalanced we experience uneasiness, sickness, pain and many other problems. When mental energy is disturbed we experience mental problems. These mental problems if left unchecked over time manifest themselves as physical problems because our organs and glands also change their normal functioning and affect the blood circulation, heartbeat and brain cells.

Today many people lead an artificial life not knowing its danger. Many of their problems are created by themselves due to their ignorance and crazy desire for too much pleasure. Many of our problems and burdens come after middle age. To understand how our problems increase with age, let us assume there is a pit about hundred feet deep with burning charcoal at the bottom. If we put a ladder and ask some people to go down one by one, those who start to go down first will not complain about the heat until they descend to a depth of 40 to 50 feet, after that they feel a certain amount of heat. When they go further down to 70 to 80 feet and reach nearer the burning charcoal they experience the sensation of burning. They try to warn those coming after them about the danger below, but no one listens. In the same manner young people say there is nothing wrong with them and they do not experience suffering. It is as we grow older and have more understanding of old age, disease and impending death that we 'begin to feel the heat'.

The Buddha says life is suffering and this is a good example for young people to understand the nature of existence. Older people also have some of this wisdom and if young people listen to them they will be able to avoid many mistakes. Here is another example for you to understand why we should listen to our elders. A flock of fishes see an unusual small obstruction in the water; it is really a trap put up by the fishermen to catch the fish. Some young fish want to go inside the obstruction and explore but the elderly fish advise them not to do that because it could be a dangerous trap. The young fish ask, 'How do we know whether it is dangerous or not? We can only know what it is if we go in and investigate'. So some of them enter and are caught in the net.

This simple example tells us that it is not necessary to have personal experience in certain things to understand whether they are good or bad. We must be prepared to accept the advice given by wise people like the Buddha who know infinitely more than we do. Therefore we should not think that we know everything and that no one can teach us about life and how to avoid its problems. When our elders and parents advise us not to do certain things, we have to listen to them, because their experience is more advanced than our theoretical knowledge regarding our worldly life. That is why parents always advise their children to do certain things and not to do other things.

'Beware of little mistake: a small leak will sink a great ship.' (Benjamin Franklin)

When young people neglect the advice given by the elders, they do many things according to their own way of thinking.

One day, the Buddha and his disciples went to a village. Some people in that village were angry with the Buddha. When they started to scold the Buddha, the disciples suggested that they go to another village to avoid the abuse. The Buddha asked, 'What guarantee is there that there won't be any disturbances in that new place?' Then the Buddha said, 'Running away is not the solution to overcome the disturbances. If we have no guilty feeling in our mind, scolding will never reach us. Therefore we must be patient and allow them to scold until they themselves get fed up.' When those people who scolded the Buddha came to know that there was no reaction from the Buddha and the disciples, they stopped their abuse after few days.

For instance having seen or having heard something that happens, some people take it so seriously as if it is a problem. Some others do not mind it and ignore it. Some others create undue fear and worry around it. Some others take it to mind and think that it is a good lesson to learn from. Others dismiss it as a joke. Some pass remarks and condemn it.

Here you can understand how the same incident is viewed in different ways by people according to their own mentality. Problems are created by our mind. If we have developed our mind to maintain patience, tolerance and understanding, we will be able not to take any incident seriously to create more problems. Our problems are of our own creation, it is not the work of others.

4

MAN AND SOCIETY

Man's unique position

One might argue that the discussion on the previous page is a very negative view of humanity, bringing down him to an inferior position and disregarding his magnificent achievements in philosophy, religion, psychology, science, the arts, architecture, literature and development of culture and the like. Far from it; in this cosmic context humans assume a unique position because they have the most rare privilege of easy possibility to salvation. It is for three reasons.

The human world has a well-balanced mixture of pleasure and pain. When pleasure is intensified (in the divine realms) or pain is predominant (in the lower worlds) one's mind does not turn towards spirituality. Buddhists maintain that extreme austerity or extreme self indulgence are not conducive to the development of wisdom and understanding. The Middle Path between extreme pleasure and austerity is advocated and the human world provides man the opportunity to tread the Middle Path. The second reason is the relative short span of human life and the unpredictability of the time of death.

Faced with imminent death one is more often inclined towards spirituality. The third reason is that while in other realms the inhabitants are mere passive recipients of the effects of their past *kamma*, man is in a favourable position to create fresh *kamma*, and is thus able to shape his own destiny.

All of this gives man the responsibility to work out his own salvation in the human plane. He is in effect his own Creator and Saviour. Many people believe that religion has come down from heaven but Buddhists know that Buddhism started on the earth and reached heaven.

What this implies is that each man has within him the Buddha-seed (potential for perfection) which he can develop without any external aid. One can become a Buddha through birth in the human plane, because it is here that he can experience existence in its entirety. Buddhists would certainly agree with Shakespeare's view of the human paradox:-

> *What a piece of work is man,*
> *how noble in reason,*
> *how infinite in faculties in form and moving;*
> *how express and admirable in action,*

how like an angel in apprehension,
how like a god: the beauty of the world,
the paragon of animals;
and yet to me what is this quintessence of dust?

~Hamlet 2:2

In many ways man is ignorant, yet he has the seed to become the highest of all beings: a fully enlightened one. Some people say that human life is between heaven and hell because the human mind can be developed easily to experience heavenly bliss, and when it is abused it could very easily experience suffering in hell. Man is man only if he has that human concern or human heartedness.

Proud man hath no heaven;
The envious man hath no neighbour;
An angry man hath not even himself.

~Chinese philosophy

'The individual by himself is helpless. Hence the social life of man which brings forth co-operative power. Man cannot be man without society. Man is one with nature.' (Greek philosopher)

In the teaching of the Buddha it is mentioned that human beings experience heavenly bliss when the objects influencing the five senses are favourable and soothing. On the other hand they also experience suffering like in hell if the objects are irritable and disturbing.

Living in harmony with others

An important ingredient for a happy life is the ability to live in harmony with others. To achieve this, we must understand that there are many paths people can take to reach the same goal. Therefore, we should not be unduly upset if other people hold to their own customs or have opinions which are different from ours.

We are living in an ever-changing world. We should not cling blindly to traditions, customs, manners, rites and rituals practised by our forefathers who adopted these practices according to their beliefs and understanding capacity prevalent at that time. Some customs or traditions handed down may be good, while others are less useful. We should consider with an open-mind whether these practices are congenial and significant to the modern world.

Some elderly people cannot tolerate the modern ideas and ways of living of the younger generation. They expect their children to follow the same age old customs and traditions of their forefathers. Instead of adopting such an attitude, they should allow the young to move with the times if the activities are harmless. However, *'There is no use whatever trying to help people who do not help themselves. You cannot push anyone up a ladder unless he be willing to climb himself.'* (Andrew Carnegie)

'If there is righteousness in the heart, there will be beauty in character. If there is beauty in character, there will be harmony in the home. If there is harmony in the home, there will be order in the nation. If there is order in the nation, there will be peace in the world'.

Allowing others the right to differ

We are also living in a world where might is stronger than right. The strong takes advantage of the weak and the rich exploits the poor. We should avoid acting in this way. If we cannot agree, we have to learn at least to agree to disagree. We should express our views gently and politely without trying to impose our views on others by force.

Those who use physical force to overcome their opponents clearly show their inability to convince the opponents as noble human beings. We find comfort in those who agree with us, but personal growth occurs in situations where there are differences in views.

Sometimes the opinion others have of our attitudes or actions may not be something we would like to hear. But if we listen to them carefully, we will see that there is some truth in those opinions. This can give us a chance for self-improvement if we are prepared to change our way of life.

The world is like a garden with different kinds of flowers. Like a bee gathering honey from a flower, we should be selective in choosing what is good and leave behind what is not useful. It is impossible to please everybody when we want to do something, because different people can have different opinions on any particular issue. You are fooling yourself if you argue with a fool.

You cannot hope to achieve peace by correcting each and every person in this world. In the same way, you cannot remove the world of stones and thorns so that the pathway may be smooth.

Likewise, we should learn to guard our senses to have peace of mind since we cannot succeed in removing disturbing objects from the world. There are many ways to correct people if they are wrong. By criticising, blaming and shouting at them publicly, you will not be able to correct them but you will only end up making them more adamant in their views.

If you speak to people tactfully in pointing out their mistakes, they are more likely to listen to you, and some day they will thank you for your guidance and kindness.

'A long dispute means both parties are wrong.' (Voltaire)

Mind your own business

It is bliss to be able to attend to our own affairs without harbouring jealousy towards others.

'One should not accuse others for mistakes and things done and left undone by them, but acknowledge one's own deeds of commission and omission.'

'He who is always observant of others' faults, and is irritable, his own defilements increase. He is far from the destruction of defilement.'

'Easy to see are the faults of others; but one's own is difficult to see. One winnows other's faults like chaff; but one's own one hides as a crafty fowler covers himself.'

(The Buddha)

No one is free from blame and criticism. The Buddha says: *'People blame others for their silence. They blame those who talk much and those who talk in moderation. There is therefore no one in this world who is not blamed.'*

Further He says: *'There never was, nor will be, nor is there now, any one who is wholly blamed or wholly praised.'*

Not all those who criticise you are your enemies. You can use the opportunity provided by their remarks to reveal the weaknesses in yourself which you cannot see. You should not give up good work just because of criticism. If you can admit your own weakness, indeed you have the intellectual strength to succeed.

We are all human

All human beings have weaknesses and are therefore prone to make mistakes. All human beings have desire, anger and ignorance. These weaknesses prevail in all of us in varying degrees. Unless you are perfect or an Arahant, you are no exception. The nature of the human mind shows itself in the following saying:- *'Man is not satisfied with his life and never finds the purpose of life even after gaining the whole world.'*

Let us take a closer look at a man who is enveloped in ignorance. His mind is clouded by disturbances, confusion and darkness. Out of ignorance, man creates misfortunes and he shares this with his fellow men. Most of the worries and miseries that come to us are due to changing worldly conditions and our own craving for worldly pleasures which to the selfish mind should continue forever.

Disappointment and unfulfilled desires which arise from unexpected changes create worry. Therefore you are responsible for your worry. Nobody is perfect in this world; everybody is liable some time to commit certain mistakes or evil actions. So how can you think that you are free from mistakes or evil? Ignorance is the main cause for nurturing the impulse of craving which in turn generates worry.

'Fear and worry disappear when ignorance is dispelled by knowledge.'

If you can understand the weaknesses present in a man's mind in this way, then there should be no reason for you to grumble over your problems. You will have the courage to face them. Man's mind is responsible for both his happiness and unhappiness.

'Nothing happens to man that is not contained within man.'—C. Jung, psychologist

All are not equally good

Occasionally, there are complaints from people who have never caused or given any trouble and yet they become innocent victims to cunning tricksters. They feel frustrated despite the good lives they have lived. They feel they have been harmed through no fault of their own. Under such circumstances, the innocent victim must realise that the world is made up of all sorts of people - the good and the not so good, the bad and the not so bad, with all the unusual characters that go to make this world of ours. The innocent victim may console himself that he belongs to the good category whereas the disturber of the peace belongs to the bad, and that on certain occasions, he will still have to bear patiently the misdeeds of the bad.

We take for instance the case of a *'good and careful driver'* and a *'bad and reckless driver.'* The good and careful driver took every precaution to drive carefully but nevertheless he met with an accident, through no fault of his own - the fault being that of a bad and reckless driver.

Thus we can see the good may have to suffer, despite their goodness, because there are bad and reckless people around us. The world is neither good nor bad. It produces criminals as well as saints, fools and enlightened ones. Out of the same clay, beautiful and ugly, useful and even useless things can be made. The quality of good pottery depends on the potter and not on the clay. The potter is in fact yourself. The moulding of your happiness or unhappiness is in your hands regardless of the circumstances around you.

Classification of men

The Buddha has classified mankind into four groups:-

1) one who works for his own good, but not for the good of others;

2) one who works for the good of others, but not for his own good;

3) one who works neither for his own good nor for the good of others; and

4) one who works for his own good as well as for the good of others.

One who works for his own good, but not for the good of others is he who strives for the abolition of evil thoughts, words and actions in himself, but he does not encourage others to abolish greed, hate and delusion.

One who works for the good of others, but not for his own good is he who encourages others to abolish evil thoughts, words and actions but does not strive for the abolition of greed, hate and delusion in himself.

One who does not work for his own good nor for the good of others is he who neither strives for the abolition of evil thoughts, words and actions in himself, nor does he encourage others to abolish greed, hatred and delusion.

One who works for his own good as well as for the good of others is he who strives for the abolition of evil thoughts, words and actions in himself, and also encourages others to abolish greed, hate and delusion. (*Anguttara Nikaya*)

Manners and customs

The standards of good manners differ among societies. In some countries, guests at dinner are expected to eat as noisily as possible. It is also not considered impolite if the guests belch at the end of the meal, since this indicates that they really enjoyed the meal. Such table manners would be considered rude, ill-mannered or uncivilised in other societies.

While in one country, putting one's finger in one's mouth or nose for any reason is considered most insulting but, it means nothing in some other countries. Some people think it is degrading to be struck by a shoe, yet among other people, a slipper can be used for spanking a child.

We discover the peculiarities of the manners and customs prevailing in other societies most acutely when travelling. We should not prejudge too quickly what is right or improper. In themselves, manners are neither good nor bad. But when they cause harm or hurt the feelings of others, then we judge an action as being good or bad manners.

We are living in an ever changing world. We should not cling blindly to the traditions, customs, manners and rituals practised by our ancestors who adopted these practices according to their circumstances. Some customs or traditions handed down by our ancestors may be good, while others are less useful or even irrelevant to modern living. We should consider with an open mind whether these practices are congenial and significant to the modern world.

In the Kalama sutta, the Buddha has given this advice about customs, traditions, beliefs and practices: 'When you know for yourself that certain things are unwholesome (*akusala*) and wrong and bad for you and others, then give them up... And when you know for yourself that certain things are wholesome (*kusala*) and good for you and others, then accept them and follow them.'

Today, some elderly people cannot tolerate the modern ideas and ways of living of the younger generation. They expect their children to follow the same age-old traditions of their forefathers. Instead of adopting such an attitude, they should allow the children to move with the times when the activities are harmless. Elders should call to mind how their own parents objected to certain popular modes of behaviour prevalent at the time when they were young. These differences in perception between the conservative parents and the younger generation are common sources of conflict within families. It does not mean that parents should hesitate to counsel and guide their children if they have gone astray due to some erroneous values. But when correcting them, it is good to remember that prevention is better than punishment. Parents should also explain to their children why certain practices are wrong, because children are not mature enough to reason why certain things are bad and certain things are good.

Discrimination against women

The Buddha says that if we are to understand anything, we must learn to 'see things as they are'. It is after such analysis of women in relation to men, that He came to the conclusion that there is no impediment in women to enable them to practise religion as men do and attain the highest state in life, which is Arahanthood or Sainthood, the highest level of mental purity. The Buddha had to face strong opposition in giving full freedom to women to practise religion.

At the time of the Buddha, before He emancipated women, the customs and traditions were such that the women were considered as chattel, to be used by men at their pleasure. Manu, the ancient law-giver of India, had decreed that women were inferior to men. Women's position in society was therefore very low, and it was restricted to the kitchen. They were not even allowed to enter temples and to participate in religious activities in any manner whatsoever.

As we have previously noted under the heading 'Birth Control', discrimination against females begins even before the child is born into this world! The widespread practice of female foeticide prevalent in many parts of the world today testifies to this horrifying fact. Further on, under the heading 'Women's Liberation Movement and its Effect on Family Life', the discrimination against women in affluent societies, particularly those aspiring for top managerial positions in the corporate sector, will be dealt with in detail.

In developing and underdeveloped countries however, the situation can only be described as being far worse and more deplorable as the following accounts will reveal. In India's ritualistic, male dominated society, widowhood is a terrible fate for a woman. There are numerous cases of widows (some still in their 20s) who were cast away from their families and shunned by society after their husbands died.

Among superstitious families, a widow often is blamed by her in-laws for her husband's death and is even ostracised. There are few options left for widows. Hindus frown on remarriage for women, although there are no such barriers for men. Until modern times, widows were expected to jump on to the funeral pyre of their husbands according to a tradition known as *suttee*. Although the practice was outlawed by the British several decades ago, the last known case occurred as recently as 1996. Most women in India have little to look forward to when they become widows.

One typical tragic example could be cited of a widow who underwent child marriage which is another custom prevalent in rural India. She laments: 'I was married off when I was only five years old. My husband, whom I never saw, was 13 and he died one month after the wedding. I am now a widow.' According to the World Bank, 65% of Indian women older than 60 are widows. That figure rises to 80% for women older than 70. The All India Democratic Women's Association reports that in India where a woman's identity is determined by her being an appendage to a male, widowhood has much larger implications than just losing a husband.

The situation is no better even in some other neighbouring countries. For a long time, families regarded daughters as inferior to sons and treated them accordingly. A girl is generally seen as suitable only for household chores. She lives through a series of social practices which generate, breed and reinforce discrimination against her. She becomes an economic burden and a moral liability. Yet, she is expected to raise healthy, hardworking and educated children and be a good mother. Many little boys grow up thinking their sisters are inferior having seen them treated less well than themselves. These beliefs are reinforced by many members of the society, including women themselves.

Perhaps the single biggest issue is the lack of support and the restrictions girls face if they want to do something with their lives beyond the traditional roles assigned to them as domestic help, baby-sitters for younger siblings, cooks and cleaners. In effect, girls are under life-long training to be good wives when they grow up. As a 16 year old girl from Rawalpindi, points out: 'Our society does not treat girls well. People here do not educate their girls because to them girls are not theirs. Girls are seen as belonging to their future in-laws' families and any investment in their future is futile. They go to their husbands' homes at a young age, usually anywhere from 13. The rest of their lives is spent looking after in-laws, and bearing and bringing up children to prolong and strengthen their husband's family line.'

We need to eradicate this type of thinking and make education compulsory and free so that it does not become an issue, she says. 'Girls should also be able to have jobs, working in places where no one disapproves and preferably with other girls so parents can't object. I have always regretted that I was born a girl. Sometimes when I was not allowed to do something I would go to my room, cry and pray to God to make me a boy.'

Although we have only given examples from India, similar stories abound in China, the Middle East, Africa and even in Europe and the Americas. The Girl Child Project in some countries is slowly changing all this by developing a core of young girls to act as catalysts in creating local awareness of the problems of girls and the discrimination they face. The issue of education crops up almost invariably. Many girls have had to fight for their right to education. Some were helped in this fight by their untutored mothers who believed that their own lives would have been better if they had had some schooling.

In many societies a woman's place is in the home; a married woman owes her first allegiance to her duties as wife and mother. There is no such thing as 'women's lib'. Even in some progressive societies women are humiliated. For example in public places, they are required not only to sit apart from the men, but out of their view – that is, behind them. When women are placed at the back of a room or hall, it acts as a subtle indication that their expected role is 'behind' and not 'together with' that of the men. Some people believe that women are prone to evil. Therefore, it would be better to get them do more domestic work so that they can forget their natural evil attitude.

Blame not others

If you learn to guard your mind properly, external happenings cannot affect you. You must not blame circumstances when things go wrong. You must not think that you are unlucky, that you are the victim of fate, or that somebody has cursed you. No matter what reason you give, you must not evade responsibility for your own actions. Try to solve your problems without sulking. Try to work cheerfully even under the most trying circumstances.

Be courageous to face any change if change is natural or necessary; so be brave enough to accept what you cannot avoid. Be wise enough to understand the uncertainty of worldly conditions which affect everybody. Therefore, you must develop courage to face disappointments and problems without feeling frustrated. Difficulties are common in our life. We have to face them bravely. If you know how to overcome them without creating further problems, you are indeed wise.

Those who try to do some service to others also face problems. They even encounter more blame than those who do not serve others at all. You should not be discouraged; instead, have the understanding to realise that selfless service eventually brings happiness as its own reward. In rendering our service to others, there must be knowledge and understanding.

Bertrand Russell, a British philosopher says;
'Love without knowledge and knowledge without love cannot produce a good life.'

Superiority of man

Among all living beings man stands out as a unique being. While his features, functions, and behaviour are classified as those of the animal world, as a human being he stands apart from all other animals. True, in the evolutionary classification, he is counted as belonging to the animal world. It is also true that very often human beings behave like animals.

Nevertheless, man is more than an animal; he is a human being, meaning, he can be kind, tender, merciful and intelligent. It is in the human being that self-consciousness operates to a high degree, and it is he, of all animals, that is endowed with the sense of right and wrong, good and evil, and with the power of judging and choosing the right and the good, and rejecting the wrong and the evil. This sense of choosing the right and the good, and acting up to it, is to be seen only in man; and that is the sense of Dharma, righteousness, which is highly spoken of in all the great religions of the world.

It is on the basis of this Dharma or righteousness that religion as well as moral life is built, and even social life becomes ennobling when its value is recognized and applied in individual as well as collective life. It is religion that holds society together. Without it, no society can live and function even for a day. It is because man has this sense of Dharma that all progress is possible for him, social as well as spiritual. And it is this special quality in him that distinguishes man from all the other animals.

'In matters of food, sleep, and other physical needs, man is on par with the animals. It is the sense of Dharma, righteous living with all its implications, that differentiates him from the animals. It is Dharma that makes a man human; without it, he is merely an animal or worse than an animal.'

Such a rare privilege as human birth should not, therefore, be wasted; it should be put to the best service, and the highest that it is capable of should be accomplished with a sense of urgency. It would be a great pity if man were to forget the real purpose of his birth and run only after mundane pleasures. A Hindu philosopher significantly remarks, *'What greater fool is there than the man who, having obtained a rare human body, neglects to achieve the real liberation of this life?'* Man should become perfect and he should manifest the nobility within. That is the purpose of all religious endeavour, the aim of all spiritual practice.

Nature of human being

Physical pleasures and material happiness are fugitive. They come and go, bringing joy and sorrow alternately. When joy comes man becomes elated, and when sorrow comes he becomes dejected. All the hopes and joys of this world are fleeting. They do not give perpetual peace or happiness to man. Uncertainty is the characteristic of this world. The whole of creation is undergoing constant and continuous change. Everything in it is subject to birth, growth, development, decay, dissolution and death. There is nothing in creation that can escape this series of transmutations.

To seek the real, which is self-revealing and immortal, man is required to turn his back on the unreal objects of this world. When he realizes the futility of running after the world and its objects, he turns his back on them. He resorts to renunciation, he withdraws himself from them and turns his search inwards. His journey ends when he reaches the 'Truth of truth' and 'Light of light'.

This turning point marks the beginning of genuine spiritual endeavour. Everything other than this is like a child's play in the name of religion. Playthings are necessary for the child, for its growth at a particular stage; but they are no longer required when that stage is past.

Religious life is an adventure. It demands an energetic spirit where occasion for doubt exists, it is right and proper for a man to doubt. The weakling or the feeble-minded cannot tread the spiritual path. 'The Self cannot be realized by the weak.' Religion offers the greatest challenge to man. It challenges him to give up too much of attachment.

No other consideration should hold man back. All the religions warn man against the dangers and pitfalls that he has to encounter in his spiritual pilgrimage. They prescribe methods by which he can avoid the pitfalls and overcome the difficulties and dangers on the way. There are several methods to suit the mental equipment and spiritual competence of diverse aspirants.

Today you may be a millionaire, tomorrow you can be a pauper. Today you are very healthy and beautiful, tomorrow the beauty and youth can vanish. Similarly you can end poverty and ill health by your Karma (deeds). This advice is a real magic that can cure all our depressed moods. It is a great tonic for weak hearts. *'Strength does not come from physical capacity. It comes from an indomitable will.'* (Mahatma Gandhi)

Man seeks wealth to satisfy his urge for pleasure. Desire seeks satisfaction; wealth helps him to get this satisfaction. If unchecked by ethical and spiritual values and disciplines, this urge for pleasure in him becomes an endless urge; every satisfaction raises ten more urges for pleasure.

'If you want a person to listen to you for a long period talk to him about himself and he will listen.'
Desires chase satisfactions and satisfaction chases desires, leaving man a prey to unethical inclination. The ideal of a complete man, integral and fulfilled, recedes far into the background. But he becomes distressed to find that his heart is still craving for pleasures; the body has become old and unfit as an instrument of pleasure, but the heart remains youthful in its urge for pleasure. This glaring fact makes him thoughtful; and, reviewing his life with its double round of pleasures, he is struck with the foolishness of it all and tries to disentangle himself from the wrong course.

'If you wish to be good, first understand that you are capable of being bad.' Spiritual progress is possible only where there is freedom of thought. Where, however, blind belief in authority prevails then there will be no mental progress. Freedom of thinking leads to mental vigour and progress, while dogmatism leads to stagnation. Experience further shows that dogmatic belief goes everywhere hand in hand with intolerance. Wherever the one appears the other is not far off.

The spiritual development of man is more important than the attainment of his material comforts. History has taught us that we cannot expect human comforts and happiness at the same time. The lives of people are in the main regulated by spiritual values and moral principles which only religion can effectively provide.

Man is the most significant of all beings, according to Buddhism; man is of more significance than the gods. Why is this? It is because the gods are merely enjoying temporarily the results of good actions performed in the past, but man contains within himself additional potentials. He is the master of his own destiny; on the battlefield of his own mind he can conquer the whole world. But in order to do this he must understand the nature of *Karma*, the principle that governs his internal and external world.

Parental responsibility

You are responsible for the well-being and upbringing of your children. If the child grows up to be a strong, healthy, and useful citizen, it is the result of your efforts. If the child grows up to be a delinquent, it is you who must bear the responsibility. Do not blame others. As parents, it is your duty to guide your child on a proper path. Although there are a few incorrigible cases of juvenile delinquency, nevertheless as parents, you are responsible for the behaviour of your children.

A child at its most impressionable age, needs the love, care, affection and attention of the parents. Without parental love and guidance, the child will be emotionally handicapped and will find the world a bewildering place to live in. Showering parental love does not mean pandering to all the demands of the child, reasonable or otherwise. Too much pampering would in fact spoil the child. The mother in bestowing her love and care, should also be strict and firm but not harsh, in handling the anger of a child. Show your love with a disciplined hand - the child will understand. Unfortunately, all too often parental love in our present day society is sadly lacking. The rush for material advancement, and the rising aspiration for equality of the sexes, have resulted in many mothers joining their husbands in the rat-race.

Mothers struggle to maintain their family image or status symbol by working in offices and shops, rather than being at home tendering to the needs of their off-spring. Children who are left to the care of relatives or paid servants, children who are left to their own devices at home, are often deprived of motherly love and care. The mother, feeling guilty about her lack of attention, would try to placate the child by giving in to all sorts of demands of the child. Such action only spoils the child.

Providing the child with sophisticated modern toys that are detrimental to character formation such as tanks, machine guns, pistols, and swords are psychologically unwholesome. The child is unwittingly being taught to condone destruction instead of being taught to be kind, compassionate and helpful. Such a child will develop brutal tendencies as it grows up. Giving a child such toys is no substitute for a parent's love and affection.

Parents are often placed in a dilemma. Rushing home from a hard day's work the weary parents have family chores waiting for them. When the day's work is done, it would be time for dinner followed by TV, and whatever time there is left, is hardly enough to attend to a child's rightful dues of parental love and affection.

With the call for women's liberation, many women seem to think that the solution is to compete with men outside the home. Such women should consider very carefully whether to bear children. It is irresponsible for a mother to bring a life into this world and then 'abandon' it. You are responsible for what you create. A child has a right to be satisfied materially, but more importantly spiritually and psychologically. The provision of material comfort is secondary compared to the provision of parental love and attention.

We know of many people from poor homes who have brought up children well with plenty of love although with a poor income. On the other hand, many rich people have provided every material comfort for their children, but being deprived of parental love, these children have grown up to become psychologically and morally handicapped.

Some women may feel that advising them to concentrate on the upbringing of the family is something degrading and reflects the thinking of the old and the conservative. It is true that in the past, women have been treated very badly, but this was due more to ignorance on the part of men than to an inherent weakness in women. The Sanskrit word for a housewife is *'Gruhini'* which literally means *'leader of the house'*. Certainly this does not imply that a woman is inferior. Rather it means a division of responsibility for the male and the female.

In certain countries, many husbands hand over their pay packet to their wives who handle domestic affairs. This leaves the man free to concentrate on what he can do best. Since each partner knows clearly what his of her responsibilities are, there is no conflict between them. The atmosphere at home is happy and peaceful where their children can grow up well.

Of course, the husband must see to it that his partner is well-cared for, that she is consulted on every family decision, that there is enough freedom for her to develop her own personality and that she has her own free time to pursue her personal interests. In this sense, husband and wife are equally responsible for the welfare of their family. They are not in competition with each other.

A mother should consider carefully whether she should continue as a working mother with all the attendant pitfalls or be a housewife giving all her due affection and care to her growing child. Strangely, some modern mothers, particularly in certain countries with military regimes facing a shortage of manpower, women are being trained to handle guns and other deadly weapons when they should be cuddling their children and training them to be good or law-abiding citizens.

The modern attitude of working mothers towards their children tends to erode the time-honoured filial piety which children are expected to uphold. The replacement of breast-feeding by bottle-feeding is yet another cause for concern. Hitherto, when mothers used to breast-feed and cuddle babies in their arms, the tender affection between mother and child was much greater.

A breast-feeding mother, through her maternal instinct, often experiences a tremendous satisfaction from knowing she is providing the baby, as nature has intended, with something of her very own which no one else can give. The influence a mother has on the child grows and becomes much more pronounced. Under such circumstances, filial piety, family cohesion and obedience are invariably present.

These traditional practices are for the good and the well-being of children. It is up to the parents, especially the mother to provide them with love, care and affection as their rightful dues. The mother is responsible for the child being good or wayward. The mother can thus reduce juvenile delinquency! At the highest level of thinking, you can see things as they are, not as you are. Then you know that you are responsible for everything.

How many youths recognize the kindness shown by parents? Usually, people do not realize it until they themselves become parents or lose their parents. We should show our gratitude through practicing filial piety by being responsible, considerate, grateful and obedient to our parents.

The man and his honey

Here is a short parable to help us to understand the real nature of life and worldly pleasure: A man had lost his way whilst he was going through a thick forest covered with thorns and rocks. Then he was confronted by a huge elephant which started to chase him. He ran for his life. While he was running he saw an old well and thought that this would be a good place for him to escape from the elephant. But very unfortunately he saw a big poisonous snake at the bottom of the well. But since there was no other way of escape from the elephant he jumped into the well and managed to cling to a thick thorny creeper that was growing on the side wall of the well. While he was hanging on to the creeper he saw two mice, a white one and a dark one. To his horror he saw that these two mice were slowly nibbling at the creeper to which he was holding on. He however found a beehive close by from which occasional drops of honey trickled down.

Facing his death in three different ways in that precarious position, he greedily started to taste the honey drops. Then someone passed by and, seeing the pathetic situation of this poor man, volunteered to give a helping hand to save his life. But this greedy and foolish man refused to listen to him because of the irresistible taste of the honey he was enjoying. The taste of the honey had intoxicated him to the point that he preferred to ignore the dangerous position he was facing.

Here in this parable, the thorny path of the forest is equated to *Samsara* (the wheel of existence). The thorny path of *Samsara* is a very uncertain and troublesome one. It is not so easy for a person to carry on his life through the rough and tough jungle of *Samsara*. The elephant here represents death. Death always follows us and makes us unhappy; our old age also creates unhappiness and insecurity in our minds. The creeper is our birth. Just as a creeper goes on growing and coiling with other plants, our birth also goes on accumulating, holding, clinging to so many other superfluous things in this world.

The two white and dark mice represent day and night respectively. From the very day that we were born to this world, the passage of day and night goes on cutting and shortening our life span. The drops of honey are the fleeting sensual worldly pleasures which tempt man to remain in this impermanent and uncertain world. The kind man who came to give his helping hand to show him the correct path and to get rid of his dangerous situation was the Buddha.

A man who thinks that it is better for him to remain in this world to enjoy worldly life without trying to attain salvation, is exactly like this foolish man who refused the offer to escape from the dangerous situation of his life just to taste a little bit of honey. Nature is evenly balanced; her equilibrium cannot be disturbed.

Natural laws, which operate unerringly and inexorably, are not swayed by praises, prayers or sacrifices. They operate at the physical and mental realms without the intervention of a law-giver. One of such natural laws which have a strong bearing on the quality of human life is the cosmic law of kamma. This law operates at the moral sphere. Wholesome and unwholesome acts performed by thought, word and deed will in due time produce their corresponding good and bad results.

If a man is cruel, performs wicked acts, and does not live in conformity with the natural cosmic laws, he pollutes the whole atmosphere with his unwholesome deeds. As a result of such unwholesome deeds, unfavourable results will arise making it difficult for him to lead a happy, contented and peaceful life. He creates unhappiness for himself and others with his polluted mind. On the other hand, if he lives in conformity with the natural cosmic law and leads a righteous and blameless life, he purifies the atmosphere with the merits of his virtues. With his positive mental vibrations, he influences those around him as well as creates an environment conducive to peace and happiness. *'Those who lead their lives by going against nature, must face the consequences either physically or mentally.'*

5

THE CORRECT ATTITUDE

The menace of drug abuse and alcoholism

Alcohol has been described as one of the prime causes of man's physical and moral degradation. Currently, another more vicious form of abuse, that of harmful and dangerous drugs, especially heroin, has created a much more serious human and social problem. This problem is now worldwide. The repercussions of drug abuse are more serious and deadly than those of alcohol. Theft, robbery, sex-related crimes and swindling of vast sums of money have occurred under the pernicious influence of drug abuse.

Drug lords, not being content as death merchants of an innocent population have even tried to control weak governments through corruption, bribery, subversion and bombings. As a matter of public policy, governments have to protect their citizens against drug abuse. Yet, drug lords in their devilish schemes have threatened the very foundation of society - human dignity. Spokesmen of conscience and their families constantly run the risk of death because they dare to cross the paths of lawless drug lords.

Without international co-operation to stamp out this evil, the vitality and the future of many nations will be bleak indeed. Worldwide, countless millions of hard-earned dollars have been spent to rid the addicts of their evil habits but the maddening craze persists.

It is our duty to help, in whatever manner we can, to eradicate this dreadful habit and to prevent our children from ever becoming victims. Life as a drug addict or an alcoholic is a life of torture and hell on earth, leading one to an early grave. It is very sad to mention that certain countries which have great religions produce great quantities of opium which they distribute all over the world.

Drunkenness

Drunkenness expels reason,
Drowns memory,
Defaces the brain,
Diminishes strength,
Inflames the blood,

*Causes external and internal incurable
wounds.*

*Is a witch to the body,
A devil to the mind,
A thief to the purse,
The beggar's curse,
The wife's woe,
The children's sorrow,
The picture of a beast,
And self murder,
Who drinks to other's health,
And robs himself of his own.*

As human beings, we should have self-control to distinguish between what is good and evil. Keep away from drug abuse and alcoholism and help others to do so. That will be the greatest service to humanity.

Failures are but the pillars of success. To learn by our failures is to achieve success. Never to have failed is never to have won. Unless we experience failure and its bitterness, we never appreciate the sweetness of victory; it becomes merely a turn of events that is of little or no interest. Failures not only help us to succeed, they make us to be alert, energetic, enthusiastic, and rich in experience.

'Many a man goes into a bar for an eye-opener and comes out blind.'

Compare not with others

You can rid yourself of unnecessary worry and trouble simply by not comparing yourself with others. As long as you regard others as your *'equal'*, *'superior'* or *'inferior'*, you will have intolerance and restlessness. If you do not adopt such an attitude, there is nothing for you to worry about. If you think you are higher than others, you may become proud. If you think you are second to none, others may descend on you. If you think you are inferior, you may lose your own self-confidence.

For most people, it is very difficult to subdue their pride. It is advisable to learn how to reduce one's pride. If you are able to sacrifice your pride, then you can find your inner peace. You can harmonise yourself with others so as to experience peace and happiness. Which is more important - to maintain your pride or peace of mind? Try to realise that equality, inferiority, and superiority are all changing relative states: you may be poor now but at another point of time you may be rich. Today you may be ignorant, later however you can become wise. Today you may be sick and unhappy but given time you will probably be healthy again. However, there are many intangible humane qualities which are regarded as mankind's heritage - human rights, human dignity, human status etc. Others have no right to deprive you of them.

'If you are good to yourself, you are good to others. If you are good to others, you are good to yourself.'

How to handle trouble-makers

You have to realise that you might have contributed something, for the troubles and problems that now befall you. It is also important for you to know what you must do to overcome the problems that have come to you through various sources. If your understanding is deep enough to overcome your responsibility for having caused the existing problem, you will certainly get the idea of how best to get rid of them.

Then you know how to handle troublemakers and your opponents. Those who oppose you also have a human heart. Therefore it is not difficult to accommodate them; develop their friendship instead of isolating them.

If you are strong enough to resist their wrong attitude, then there is no reason to avoid associating with them. Through your association with such people, you can influence them for their own betterment. Remember that it is your own understanding that protects you from your enemies and allows you to guide them to become good.

If a man does something wrong to you through his ignorance or misunderstanding, that is the most opportune time for you to show your wisdom, your education and religious understanding.

What is the use of all your education and your religious knowledge if you have not learned how to behave yourself as a real gentleman particularly at a time of trial? When others do wrong to you, you must regard their action as an opportunity for you to develop your patience and sympathy.

Patience is one of the prime qualities which everyone must cultivate. The more you practise such a virtue, the more you will be able to maintain your dignity. You must know how to make good use of your knowledge and principles to deal with people who are hostile to you.

Sooner or later, they will realise their folly and change their hostile attitude. Sometimes, people try to take advantage of your tolerance and patience as signs of weakness. That is the time for you to act wisely without becoming a victim to such cunning people. Kindness, honesty, and patience are fertile grounds for cunning people to take advantage to their own benefit.

Progress and pollution

While scientific knowledge rendered man a skeptic alienated from his cultural heritage, technology robbed him of his creative ability. The machine with its vast powers of production has reduced man to a button pusher and has thrown millions of workers out of employment. Their muscular and creative powers have been left unharnessed, thwarted and frustrated. As a result the indigenous folk arts and crafts of all nations, which were in fact expressions of sublimated emotions, became almost extinct. Man in his admiration for creativity and feeble struggle for self-expression has now become an antique collector.

Having thus briefly outlined the main causes responsible for modern social trends, it is useful to glance at their effects. HIV & AIDS have become rampant; it is reported that there was an increase of 300% within one decade in the United States. The ever widening field of psychiatry shows that mental health is rapidly deteriorating. Alcoholism and drug addiction are major health problems.

The crime rate is ever mounting. Bonds of wedlock have become sadly brittle and the divorce rate is alarmingly high. The family as a viable institution is threatened, according to some sociologists, and even extinction is predicted in the not too distant future.

Disruption of family life has affected child life most pathetically.

A British report of Health Economics informs us that babies are the most common homicide victims in Britain. They are battered to death at times of family stress. Teenage drug addictions and juvenile delinquency have become alarming problems of the day. These social phenomena are directly related to man's attitude towards sense pleasure and serious rethinking and re-education seems most urgent today if man is to be saved from the imminent danger of self- destruction through sensuality.

Marital bonds of modern man are so brittle and fragile because these cohesive emotional forces are lost in sensuality. Much emphasis is laid on carnal pleasure while personality adjustments and emotional involvement which call for sacrifices and selflessness respectively, are ignored or neglected. Though sex is an important basic requirement in marriage, it is not the most important aspect of family life. Indulgence in sex for its own sake never brings satisfaction, whence fulfillment? The insatiability of lust is disdainfully illustrated in Buddhist literature by the traditional simile of a dog licking a bone to satisfy hunger. But sex as an expression of conjugal love is a satisfying emotional experience.

If sex was the only concern, man need not have evolved an institution like the family. Animals too satisfy their sex instinct, but nothing comparable to the human family has evolved in the animal kingdom. The important function of family life seems to be to teach man a great moral lesson to overcome his egocentric nature.

Parents start life in their mothers' wombs as the most selfish parasites. They then pass through the emotional stages of self-love, conjugal love and parental love. As mature people and a parents they completely lose themselves in the service of their offspring. Their self-denial is such they even relinquish their personal possessions, acquired through the toil of a lifetime. Finally they make an emotional self- sacrifice when they get a partner for their child to love and cherish. In old age they regard their offspring with equanimity and contentment. This emotional maturity and fulfillment is utterly impossible if sensuality is regarded as the goal of married life.

Committing suicide

Suicide is the act of intentionally and voluntarily taking one's own life. Suicides fall into two types; conventional and personal. The first type occurs as a result of tradition and the force of public opinion. An example is *hara-kiri*, the ritualistic suicide committed by abdominal stabbing by a Japanese man of rank when he faced disgrace.

Personal suicides are more typical of modern times. The theory is generally accepted that suicide is a result of failure to adjust to one's life stresses and strains. Suicide is a way to solve various types of personal problems – loneliness, rejection, hate, desire for revenge, fear, physical pain, feelings of guilt etc. More men commit suicide than do women, and this applies to all age groups. However, women make more unsuccessful attempts than do men, either because of lack of skill in the art of killing or because of emotional differences.

Most people who commit suicide are depressed. The highest incidence occurs in those whose depression is accompanied by a pervasive sense of hopelessness and a loss of interest or pleasure in activities. In addition, people who are older, single, divorced or widowed, and especially those who are addicted to alcohol or drugs, are at higher risk. Those who are homeless are also more serious suicide risk takers than others.

Teenage suicide, particularly is a frightening problem. The suicide rate has doubled in adolescent males. For various reasons, however, a similar rise has not occurred in females.

Some experts feel that the rise in teenage suicides is due to the complexity and stress of modern life. It is also known that some television dramas and news stories about suicide produce a seasonal rise in the number of youngsters who take their lives. Unemployment and pressure to achieve are also factors.

What can we do to prevent someone's suicide? There are several warning signals to watch for, including withdrawal from the company of friends and from regular activities; neglect of personal appearance; radical changes in eating and sleeping habits; and abuse of drugs and alcohol. Some teenagers make their intentions even more obvious. They may give away cherished possessions or say: 'I won't be a problem much longer'. The actual act of suicide often follows some emotional loss such as a break with a girlfriend (or boyfriend) or a family divorce.

Hence, if you should spot any of these behaviour changes – and they must be taken seriously – you should immediately discuss your child's unhappiness with him. For instance, ask specific and direct questions about what he is planning to do. Bringing things out in the open may reduce his anxiety, and he will sense your support. Only then may you be able to attack the problem itself and seek professional help if necessary.

The permissiveness of modern society, which implies greater tolerance of deviant behaviour may partly be responsible for the increase in suicidal acts, especially through poisoning. Society's attitude toward suicidal behaviour has grown less moralistic and punitive. There is now a greater readiness to understand rather than to condemn, but a tendency to conceal suicidal acts still persists. A fatal suicidal act tends to cause grief reactions and guilt feelings on the part of those who may feel that they could have prevented by caring and loving more than they did. Unsatisfied craving or failure to gain what people want can cause suicide. No religion has ever condoned this cruel act.

The telephone is now commonly used as a means of communication among lonely and desperate individuals contemplating suicide, and seeking support and advice from members of a caring society. As in the case of 'Alcoholics Anonymous' and other similar organizations, voluntary workers serve as advisers round the clock and their services are available to would-be suicidal cases at any time. There is evidence that this kind of service does help to avert suicidal acts to a great extent.

Mutual understanding

Remember that whatever happens, you cannot feel hurt if you know how to maintain a balanced frame of mind. You are hurt only by the mental attitude that you adopt towards yourself and towards others. If you show a loving attitude towards others, you will likewise receive a loving attitude. If you show hate, you will undoubtedly receive hate in return.

An angry man breathes out poison, and he hurts himself more than he would hurt others.

An angry man who shouts at others will be unable to see things in a proper perspective as if smoke got into his eyes. Anyone who is wise not to be angered cannot be hurt. Always remember that no one can hurt you unless you pave the way for others to do so. If you follow the Dhamma (righteous way of life), that Dhamma will protect you. The Buddha says:-

'Whoever harms a harmless person, one who is pure and guiltless, upon that very fool the evil recoils like fine dust thrown against the wind.' Dhammapada.

If you arouse the anger of others you are responsible for the reaction it produces. By showing your aggressive attitude, you will only fulfill the wishes of your enemies. Unity and harmony are most important aspect in our lives. *'When spider webs unite, they can tie up a lion'.*

Your responsibility

You must learn how to protect whatever inner peace and calm you have created within your mind. To preserve the inner peace, you must know when to reduce your superiority complex; you must also know when to ignore your pride, when to subdue your false ego, when to discard you adamance and when to practise patience. You should not allow others to take away your inner peace. You can preserve your inner peace if you know how to act wisely.

Wisdom comes through understanding. *'Man is a rising animal.'* Scientists say it has taken millions of years for us to stand today as humans. Use your full effort with conviction to stand by your principles firmly and gently. At the same time, be humble for the sake of peace and tolerance to avoid clashes and violence. By doing so you will never lose anything. Instead, you gain in the end.

If we wish to bring peace to the world, we must start by changing our wrong attitude and selfishness. World peace stems from inner peace. We must learn how to guard ourselves against unjust criticism and how to make sensible use of constructive criticism. We must always look objectively at criticism. If the criticism levelled at us is unjust, ill-founded, given with a bad intention, we should not surrender our dignity in a cowardly manner.

If we know that there is no conscious guilt in us, our attitude is correct and appreciated by wise people, then we need not worry about ill-founded criticism. Our understanding of both constructive and destructive criticism is important for us to adjust our way of life to live in any society. We are all inclined to blame others for our own shortcomings and misfortunes. Have you ever given a thought that you yourself could be also responsible for your own problems?

Your sorrow has nothing to do with a family curse or the original sin of an ancestor. Neither is it the work of a god or a devil. Your sorrow is of your own making. You are therefore your own jailor and your own liberator. You create your own hell and your own heaven. You have the potential to become a sinner or a saint. No other person can make you a sinner or a saint.

You must learn to shoulder the responsibilities of your own life. You have to learn to admit your own weaknesses without blaming or disturbing others. Remember the old saying:-

'The uncultured man always blames others; the semi-cultured man blames himself and the fully-cultured man blames neither.'

Whenever any problem arises, we as understanding people should try to find out ourselves where the mistake lies without blaming anybody. If each person could try to correct himself, there would not be any trouble or conflict in this world. But people just do not make the effort to improve their understanding by acting without bias. They prefer to find scapegoats. They look outside of themselves for the source of their troubles because they are reluctant to admit their own weaknesses.

Man's mind is given to so much self-deceit that he will try to find some excuse to justify his action so as to create an illusion that he is blameless. The Buddha says:- *'Easily seen are other's faults; hard indeed it is to see one's own faults.'* Dhammapada

To hide their weaknesses with disclaimers for mistakes, many people adopt an aggressive attitude towards others thinking that by so doing, they can avoid the shameful situation or the cause of the complaint against them. They do not realise that such an attitude would only create more problems for themselves besides giving rise to an unhealthy atmosphere all around.

You must admit when you are wrong, do not follow the ways of the uncultured who always blame others. The Buddha further says:-

'The fool who does not admit he is a fool, is a real fool. And the fool who admits he is a fool is wise to that extent.' Dhammapada.

You are responsible for the sorrow that comes to you. When you allow even minor incidents to disturb your mind, that in itself will give rise to your sorrow. You must understand that it is not that something is wrong with the world, but that something is wrong with our way of life when we suffer.

Expect nothing and nothing will disappoint you

You can avoid disappointments by not having any expectations with regard to your honour. If you expect nothing, then nothing can disappoint you and nothing can be taken from you. Do something for the benefit of others to relieve suffering. If you can do that without expecting any kind of reward, then you can have no cause of disappointment. You can be a contented person! The happiness that appears in your mind for the good that you have done, is itself a big reward.

That happiness creates immense satisfaction in your life. By expecting rewards, you not only miss your happiness, but very often you will even experience bitter disappointment. And not wanting anything is the best weapon you can have to protect yourself from those who wish to harm you. There is a saying, 'Beware the man who does not want anything'.

Perhaps, you may be a person who is good by nature and so you do not harm others. But nevertheless you get blamed despite having done good. Then you might ask, 'If good begets good and bad begets bad, why should I have to suffer when I am completely innocent? Why should I have to undergo so many difficulties? Why should I be troubled with so many disturbances? Why should I get blamed by others despite my good work?' The simple answer is that when you do some good deeds you may unwittingly be going against many evil forces at work in this world.

Those evil forces naturally interrupt good deeds. If not, it could be that you are facing the evil effects of some past evil deeds *(kamma)* that is ripening at the present moment. By continuing your good work with sound understanding, you will eventually be free from such troubles. Since you are the one who initially created the disappointments, it is reasonable that only you can overcome them by realising the true situation of your worldly life.

Many of the worldly conditions are beyond our control. Unexpected changes, diverse influences and uncertainties do occur to disappoint us. That is why it is sometimes difficult to do good in such changing circumstances. If people think of this advice of the Buddha, everybody could contribute something for their mutual protection. To be a poor, content, and happy person is better than being one who is rich, worried, and afflicted with greed.

Some people grumble by saying that we have done so much for them but they did not say even 'thank you'. Why is gratitude so important if we can experience happiness by helping others?

The Buddha considered gratitude to be a great virtue. However, it is true that this virtue is rare in any society. You cannot always expect other people to be grateful to you for what you have done. People are inclined to be forgetful especially when it comes to remembering past favours. If people fail to show gratitude, you have to learn to accept them as such - only then can you avoid disappointment. You can be happy regardless of whether people are grateful for your kindness and help; you need only think and feel satisfied that you have done your noble duty as a human being to your fellow men.

Forgive and forget

To take revenge on troublemakers is only to create more problems and disturbances. You must realise that negative feelings and hostile actions could only bring harm and suffering to both you and the troublemaker. In order to take retaliatory action, you have to harbour intense hatred in your heart. This hatred is like a poison. Since the poison is initially in you, surely it will harm you before it can harm anyone else. Before you can throw a blazing iron at another, you get burned first. Your action merely goes to show that there is no basic difference between you and your opponent.

By hating others, you only give them power over you. You do not solve your problem. If you become angry with a person who simply smiles back at you, then you will feel defeated and miserable. Since he did not co-operate with you to fulfil your wish, it is he who is victorious. The Buddha teaches us how to live happily when we are faced with disturbances. *'Ah happily do we live without hate amongst the hateful. Amidst hateful men, we live without hate.'* *Dhammapada*

We can live happily without fanning the fires of hatred. Perhaps you may not be strong enough to extend compassionate love to your enemies; but for the sake of your own health and happiness and that of everybody else, you must at least learn how to forgive and forget.

By not hating or crushing your troublemaker, you act like a gentleman. To act in this manner, you must understand that the other person has been misled by anger, jealousy and ignorance. He is therefore no different from all other human beings who have also at one time or another been misled by the same negative states of mind.

The Buddha says:- *'Evil-doers are not wicked by nature. They do evil because they are ignorant.'* Therefore they need guidance.

We should not curse them. It is not justifiable for us to say that they should be condemned to everlasting suffering as it is never too late to correct them. We should try to explain to them in a very convincing way that they are in fact in the wrong. With this understanding, you can treat the evil-doer as you would a patient who is suffering from a sickness and in need of treatment. When the sickness is cured the ex-patient and everyone else will be well and happy. The ignorant must be guided by the wise. *'Good life is inspired by love and guided by knowledge.'*

If a man does something wrong to you because of ignorance or misunderstanding, then that is the time to radiate your compassionate love towards the evil-doer. One day, he will realise this folly and relent his evil habits. So it is better to give him a chance to be good. Repentance of his past misdeeds will change him into a better person and in the end he will truly appreciate your kind thoughts. The compassionate Buddha's advice is:

> *'Hatred does not cease by hatred;*
> *by love alone it ceases.*
> *This is an eternal law.'* Dhammapada

If you can radiate compassionate love, no harm will come to you. This will help you to achieve both physical and mental health. Life has its own rhythm. When you lose on the swing, you gain on the roundabout. Those who do not understand this principle often get into trouble and face difficulties in life.

If a man does something wrong to you again and again, you must act wisely in correcting him each time he makes the mistake. Although it is not so easy to do that, you should nevertheless try your best to follow the example set by the Buddha. Then you will come to know that it is after all not impossible. The attitude of the Buddha in such a situation could be summarised thus:- *'The more evil that comes to me, the more good will radiate from me.'*

Some people think that it is not practicable to return good for evil. Try it and see for yourself. If you find it too difficult to return good for evil, then you can still do a great service to yourself and to others by at least not returning evil for evil.

'Sympathetic consideration is needed for less-understanding people who make mistakes.'

How to reduce your mental agony

There is in fact nothing perfectly bad or perfectly good in this world because the very things that are welcomed by one group could be hated by another group. Therefore, we define good and bad according to our needs. Things are neither good nor bad by nature. According to Buddhism, the world exists on conflict to which we are a part. *'I have never in my life learned anything from any man who agreed with me.'* (Dudley Field Malone)

If we have strong selfish cravings for existence and the senses, we will have to pay the price for our wrong views of the world. Wishful thinking, yearnings for eternity and clinging to feelings such as the elusive 'I' or 'Me' only warp the mind and its sense of time. Unfulfilled desires yield their crop of quarrels, friction, communication failures, fear, worry, loneliness and anxiety. There are no free rides.

If you are desirous of eradicating the mental agony within you, you have to subdue selfish cravings. Life's journey depends on whether you take the right path and develop yourself spiritually to unwind the tensions of worldly life or you continue to indulge in sensual pleasures with their many attendant confrontations.

One way to relieve yourself of your occasional mental agony is to understand the degree of your own sufferings and difficulties compared with those experienced by others. When you are unhappy, you often feel that the world is against you or everything around you is wrong. However, if you take a mental note of things around you and count your blessings, surprisingly, you will find that you are indeed much better off than many other people.

You have been unduly exaggerating your own difficulties and problems. Others are in fact worse off, and yet they do not worry themselves unduly. If you face any problems, you should try to solve them instead of worrying and creating mental anguish within you. The Chinese have a practical saying about solving problems:-

'If you have a big problem, try to reduce it to a small problem. If you have a small problem, try to reduce it to no problem.'

Another way to reduce your problems is to think what you have gone through before, under similar or even worse circumstances; and how you have, through your own patience, initiative and effort, been able to surmount your then seemingly unavoidable difficulties. By doing so, you will not permit your existing problems to 'drown you'. On the contrary, by seeing life in a new perspective you will be able to solve whatever problems that you may now face.

You should realise that you have gone through much worse situations before and that you are prepared to face them directly, come what may. With this frame of mind, you will soon regain your self-confidence and be in a better position to solve whatever problems that will be in store for you.

If you are facing a problem, there must surely be a remedy to overcome it. So why worry? On the other hand, even if there is no solution for your problem, again why worry because your worry cannot contribute anything to settle your problem!

The increase of all kinds of mental ailments and disturbances is the most alarming of all diseases of the modern age. There are more and more mentally sick patients all over the world especially in affluent countries.

In many cases the criminal element within our society is mentioned in the same breath as mental illness. One positive and far-reaching result directly from the research work of Freud, is the recognition that criminals and delinquents are mentally sick people, who need treatment rather than punishment. It is this liberal outlook on the problem that is the basis of all 'progressive' social reform to replace punishment with rehabilitation.

When we do not see how other people live, we may not learn the different ways of living. Personal encounters with people different from ourselves make us feel more sympathetic. Intolerance is often born of ignorance of another person's needs and way of thinking.

Change yourself

What can you achieve by changing the world? Can you achieve perfection? Never, you will only be able to feed your vanity and fulfil your ego. You will be bound to the wheel of existence. But by changing yourself, by realising the nature of self through selflessness, self-discipline and self-exertion, you can achieve perfection.

By achieving such perfection, your life becomes meaningful and you can render great service to others. People will be inspired by your example; they will follow you and also achieve the common aim in life. This is why one man, Siddharta, who wanted to become a Buddha gave up his kingdom in order to become an ascetic. By becoming a king he would have served only his subjects, but by transforming himself through self effort, he was able to save the world. Man today is the result of millions of past thoughts and actions. He is not ready-made for he 'becomes and continues becoming'. His character is determined by his own thinking process. Man is not perfect by nature; he has to train himself to be perfect.

Life does not belong to human beings alone. Many other life forms exist in this universe. However, human beings have a greater thinking and reasoning power. In that respect they are superior to other living beings since they have the intelligence to mould their way of life in order to get rid of their worldly sufferings. Hence, if the purpose of life is just to get rid of sufferings, then human beings can achieve that end through their own effort. But life will be a failure if it is not used properly. The Buddha stresses the value of being a human. He painted the most perfect picture of a human being striving and struggling from life to life in his quest for perfection.

In fact, life is an unique experience. There is nothing with which to compare it; no measure of its value could be determined in terms of some other things, and money cannot purchase it. Yet, many have not learned what to do with this 'priceless pearl'. Life does not mean mere physical body or senses, but the thinking human mind.

Make the best use of life

The important point about life is that we have it and therefore we must make the best use of it. This indeed is the great value of life, the opportunity of making the maximum use of it. Many people lead narrow, unhappy and depressed lives because they do not try to make the best use of life. They spend most of the time worrying and struggling for survival, working like slaves, confronting enormous problems and hindrances.

We spend enormous amounts of energy in an emotional battlefield – fighting for survival, fighting for power, fighting for gain, fighting for name, fighting for pleasure and fighting to be free from danger. Occasionally, we do gain a little bit of momentary satisfaction but every pleasure inevitably ends with suffering.

Look at the world and you can see how people are fighting against each other, bombing, hijacking, and harming one another. The whole world is like a mad house. People have forgotten their good human character and have allowed crookedness, cruelty, cheating, robbing, harbouring of anger, grudge, greed and ignorance to reign over them. Apparently there is no room in man's mind to cultivate good thoughts. How then can one find peace, happiness and contentment in a battlefield in which one is continually fighting either for gain or escape from danger? 'Man's inhumanity to man makes countless thousands mourn.'

If you can understand the real nature of life and the world, then you can readily understand why it is absolutely necessary to attain liberation and you would not delay your effort for attainment of this blissful state. Today you are fighting to escape from suffering through a worldly way, which is temporary. However, if you try to get rid of your suffering by developing the spiritual aspect of your life, then you can find real peace.

When you protect yourself you protect others

People must learn to cure themselves from false views and the universal madness at the individual level, before there can be peace and harmony in the family and society and sanity globally. It is at the individual level that we have to watch our minds with awareness, and by so doing protect ourselves and others at the same time. The Dhammapada says:

'If you hold yourself dear, watch yourself well.'

The need to watch ourselves well by practising mindfulness is illustrated by an analogy given by the Buddha, of the acrobat and a boy. Once there was an acrobat who performed dangerous acts with his pupil. A slip on either his part or by his pupil could bring injury. In one of his acts, he climbed his bamboo pole and told his pupil: 'Now boy, climb the pole and stand on my shoulders.' After the boy had done that, the master said: 'Now boy, protect me and I will protect you; by looking after each other, we will show our tricks, earn money and come down safe from the pole.' The pupil thought for a moment and then replied: 'No master, that won't do. Why don't you protect yourself and I will protect myself. Thus self-protected and self-guarded we will show our tricks, earn money, and come down safe from the pole. This is the method.' According to the Buddha, just as the pupil had said to his master: 'I will protect myself', so should we practise mindfulness to protect ourselves. This practice will also protect others. By protecting oneself, one protects others; by protecting others, one protects oneself. And he does this by repeated practice, development and frequent occupation with tolerance, harmlessness, loving-kindness and compassion. Therefore, by practising these virtues, which can only be cultivated with mindfulness, one brings protection and security to others.

We must not misunderstand by thinking that the act of serving oneself is egoism and selfishness. By serving oneself, we do not mean giving vent to our greed, since this is not, in the truest sense, service to oneself. Serving oneself means that one should practice self-discipline, moral and mental training. While practising these qualities, one is doing the highest service to others. In addition, how can one be of real service to others if one is morally and mentally weak?

We serve ourselves and others by avoiding evil, doing good, and purifying our mind. This is the crux of what all Buddhas teach. To avoid evil is to refrain from doing acts which are motivated from unwholesome mental roots, that is greed, hatred and delusion. On the other hand, we constantly strive with right effort to act out of compassion and wisdom. This is what is meant by doing good. We purify our minds by reducing and finally eradicating unwholesome thoughts in the mind. In addition, we extend our thoughts of universal love and kindness to all beings without discrimination. We radiate goodwill to all beings and wish that they are well and happy, free from harm and danger and free from pain and suffering.

May you all be well and happy!
May you and all your problems be ended!

"While we have witnessed dazzling achievements on a materialistic level in the twentieth century, we have unfortunately not been able to attain peace and happiness on a mental level. The human race is beset by a growing number of problems which can only be solved by paying more attention to our spiritual development."

This book is aimed at examining **the most common problems** which beset us today as parents, **husbands, wives, children,** in our daily lives.

- Expect nothing and nothing will disappoint you
- When you protect yourself you protect others
- You are responsible for your inner peace
- World is nothing but a series of waves
- You create your own heaven and hell
- Life is not free from suffering
- The world is a battlefield
- Compassionate love
- Blame not others
- Be unbiased
- Diplomacy

*"**W**herever the Buddha's teachings have flourished,*
either in cities or countrysides,
people would gain inconceivable benefits.
The land and pepole would be enveloped in peace.
The sun and moon will shine clear and bright.
Wind and rain would appear accordingly,
and there will be no disasters.
Nations would be prosperous
and there would be no use for soldiers or weapons.
People would abide by morality and accord with laws.
They would be courteous and humble,
and everyone would be content without injustices.
There would be no thefts or violence.
The strong would not dominate the weak
and everyone would get their fair share."

THE BUDDHA SPEAKS OF
THE INFINITE LIFE SUTRA OF
ADORNMENT, PURITY, EQUALITY
AND ENLIGHTENMENT OF
THE MAHAYANA SCHOOL 👁

With bad advisors forever left behind,
From paths of evil he departs for eternity,
Soon to see the Buddha of Limitless Light
And perfect Samantabhadra's Supreme Vows.

The supreme and endless blessings
of Samantabhadra's deeds,
I now universally transfer.
May every living being, drowning and adrift,
Soon return to the Pure Land of
Limitless Light!

~The Vows of Samantabhadra~

I vow that when my life approaches its end,
All obstructions will be swept away;
I will see Amitabha Buddha,
And be born in His Western Pure Land of
Ultimate Bliss and Peace.

When reborn in the Western Pure Land,
I will perfect and completely fulfill
Without exception these Great Vows,
To delight and benefit all beings.

~The Vows of Samantabhadra
Avatamsaka Sutra~

NAME OF SPONSOR
助印功德芳名

書　名：You & Your Problems
Book Serial No.,書號：EN177

N.T.Dollars：

5,000：〔周子沛、周陳時〕。周陳時。

3,133：王金平。

1,200：謝凱琳。

1,000：〔枋三雄、枋陳貝、枋怡君、枋政緯、枋直億〕。
　　　　STBLLA SISA JOSB DBRRATI。

　783：王珠慶。

　752：邵淑貞。陳瑞祥。

　750：陳光雄設計規劃有限公司。

　626：三寶弟子。

　470：林育鵬。

　376：吳淑媛。陳滿女。

　314：蕭淑娥。林金菊。林姿良。

　188：林伯紹。張素黎。洪麗姿。余明賢。薛文典。林耘朵。
　　　　木梵師。李志浦。^{亡者}林瑞華。

　157：陳瓊娥。黃煜弘。洪順喜。張錫智。

　78：黃懷寬。陳美秀。陳春福。陳科穎。陳揚升。李美枝。
　　　　張祐瑋。陳碩民。陳瓊鑾。洪雍雯。洪瑞玲。鄭有成。
　　　　顏廷安。黃柏穎。黃柏誠。

41,850：佛陀教育基金會。
The Corporate Body of the Buddha Educational Foundation。

Total: N.T.Dollars 67,500 , 2,500 copies.
以上合計：台幣 67,500 元，恭印 2,500 冊。

DEDICATION OF MERIT

May the merit and virtue
accrued from this work
adorn Amitabha Buddha's Pure Land,
repay the four great kindnesses above,
and relieve the suffering of
those on the three paths below.

May those who see or hear of these efforts
generate Bodhi-mind,
spend their lives devoted to the Buddha Dharma,
and finally be reborn together in
the Land of Ultimate Bliss.
Homage to Amita Buddha!

NAMO AMITABHA
南無阿彌陀佛

財團法人佛陀教育基金會　印贈
台北市杭州南路一段五十五號十一樓
Printed and donated for free distribution by
The Corporate Body of the Buddha Educational Foundation
11F., 55 Hang Chow South Road Sec 1, Taipei, Taiwan, R.O.C.
Tel: 886-2-23951198 , Fax: 886-2-23913415
Email: overseas@budaedu.org
Website:http://www.budaedu.org

This book is strictly for free distribution, it is not for sale.
Printed in Taiwan
2,500 copies; July 2007
EN177-6588